The Game-Centred Approach to Sport Literacy

The Game-Centred Approach (GCA) is the ideal framework for coaches and teachers to develop comprehensive tactical or technical lessons for any game, both in physical education and in extracurricular sport contexts. Learning about the pedagogical models included in this approach has never been easier thanks to this short introductory guide.

The book helps the reader acquire the skills needed to design effective session plans, regardless of the sport that is being taught or coached. It introduces the core concepts underpinning the GCA model, complemented by practical examples of tasks and strategies for each game category and assessment instrument.

This is essential reading for all educators, coaches or sports professionals who wish to improve their teaching or coaching to enhance their students' and players' physical literacy and sport competence. It is also invaluable reading for any student or researcher working in physical education, sport coaching or sport pedagogy.

Sixto González-Víllora is currently an Associate Professor and Dean (2016–2020) in the Faculty of Education at the University of Castilla-La Mancha, Spain. His research focuses on models-based practice, teacher learning/research and youth sport.

Javier Fernandez-Rio is currently an Associate Professor in the Faculty of Teacher Training and Education at the University of Oviedo, Spain. He has co-authored chapters in two Taylor & Francis books: *Digital Technologies in Physical Education* and *Cooperative Learning in Physical Education*.

Eva Guijarro is a PhD candidate in the Faculty of Education at the University of Castilla-La Mancha, Spain. Her research interests include pedagogical models and the evaluation of different variables relevant in the physical education context and extracurricular sports.

Manuel Jacob Sierra-Díaz is a physical education teacher and researcher. Currently, he is a PhD candidate in the Faculty of Education at the University of Castilla-La Mancha, Spain. He is investigating the psychosocial outcomes in different models-based practices.

Routledge Focus on Sport Pedagogy
Series editor
Ash Casey
Loughborough University, UK

The field of sport pedagogy (physical education and coaching) is united by the desire to improve the experiences of young people and adult participants. The *Routledge Focus on Sport Pedagogy* series presents small books on big topics in an effort to eradicate the boundaries that currently exist between young people, adult learners, coaches, teachers and academics, in schools, clubs and universities. Theoretically grounded but with a strong emphasis on practice, the series aims to open up important and useful new perspectives on teaching, coaching and learning in sport and physical education.

Perspectives on Game-Based Coaching
Edited by Shane Pill

The Game-Centred Approach to Sport Literacy
Sixto González-Víllora, Javier Fernandez-Rio, Eva Guijarro and Manuel Jacob Sierra-Díaz

For more information about this series, please visit: www.routledge.com/Routledge-Focus-on-Sport-Pedagogy/book-series/RFSPED

The Game-Centred Approach to Sport Literacy

Sixto González-Víllora,
Javier Fernandez-Rio,
Eva Guijarro and
Manuel Jacob Sierra-Díaz

LONDON AND NEW YORK

First published 2021
by Routledge
2 Park Square, Milton Park, Abingdon, Oxon OX14 4RN

and by Routledge
605 Third Avenue, New York, NY 10017

First issued in paperback 2022

Routledge is an imprint of the Taylor & Francis Group, an informa business

© 2021 Sixto González-Víllora, Javier Fernandez-Rio, Eva Guijarro and Manuel Jacob Sierra-Díaz

The rights of Sixto González-Víllora, Javier Fernandez-Rio, Eva Guijarro and Manuel Jacob Sierra-Díaz to be identified as authors of this work has been asserted by them in accordance with sections 77 and 78 of the Copyright, Designs and Patents Act 1988.

All rights reserved. No part of this book may be reprinted or reproduced or utilised in any form or by any electronic, mechanical, or other means, now known or hereafter invented, including photocopying and recording, or in any information storage or retrieval system, without permission in writing from the publishers.

Trademark notice: Product or corporate names may be trademarks or registered trademarks, and are used only for identification and explanation without intent to infringe.

Publisher's Note
The publisher has gone to great lengths to ensure the quality of this reprint but points out that some imperfections in the original copies may be apparent.

British Library Cataloguing-in-Publication Data
A catalogue record for this book is available from the British Library

Library of Congress Cataloging-in-Publication Data
A catalog record for this book has been requested

ISBN 13: 978-0-367-56757-6 (pbk)
ISBN 13: 978-0-367-44043-5 (hbk)
ISBN 13: 978-1-00-300725-8 (ebk)

DOI: 10.4324/9781003007258

Typeset in Times New Roman
by Apex CoVantage, LLC

Contents

Prologue   vi
List of figures   vii
List of tables   viii
Series editor foreword   x

1. Building the Game-Centred Approach: a historical overview, implementation and transference   1

2. Practical application of invasion/territory games using the Tactical Games Approach   23

3. Practical applications of net/wall games using Game Sense   40

4. Practical application of the Developmental Game Stage Model on striking/fielding games   58

5. Practical applications of Teaching Games for Understanding on target games   72

6. Practical application of Play Practice on individual games   92

7. Future perspectives in Game-Centred Approaches: hybridizations   112

Analytical index   130
Practical sessions index   136

Prologue

The Game-Centred Approach to Sport Literacy provides a comprehensive introduction to the main ideas and practices of this approach to physical education and sport. The authors have sport coaches principally in mind, but their accessible and readable style will make this book a primary resource for all practitioners in the physical education and sport pedagogy field. The first and last chapters act as theoretical bookends to five more chapters that explore the practical application of the Game-Centred Approach in invasion/territory games, net/wall games, striking/fielding games, target games and individual games. In the first chapter the authors explain the main ideas behind the Game-Centred Approach in accessible language, dealing with some of the complex issues in games coaching and teaching in a readable style. The final chapter takes up the issue of hybridization within a Game-Centred Approach, where games teaching and learning is combined with other pedagogical models such as sport education and cooperative learning to create hybrids. The five practical application chapters provide rich details of practices for coaches, carefully explained and illustrated with diagrams where appropriate. The book draws on the most up-to-date research literature in the physical education and sport pedagogy field so readers and users can be assured that best practice is being advocated. Again, the authors deal with great facility often complex research literature and issues such as assessment and fidelity. This book is a good illustration of the advances that have been made with the Game-Centred Approach since the early work of Thorpe, Bunker and Almond at Loughborough University. It will be a key resource for all serious games coaches and teachers.

Professor David Kirk
University of Strathclyde
February 2020

Figures*

1.1	Shift from traditional approach to athlete/student-centred pedagogies.	4
1.2	Main features of GCAs.	5
2.1	Practice task 4v2 in a 10x10 metres playing area.	33
2.2	Game 1. 3v3 played in a 30x15 metres playing area divided by zones (A, B and C).	34
3.1	Base position game.	49
3.2	Searching for the "Os." Laterality game.	51
4.1	*Balls to the Box.*	64
4.2	*Tag the Runner.*	67
5.1	TGfU structure in target games.	78
5.2	The shootball game.	85
6.1	A modified game of the familiarization of dorsal flotation in a deep swimming pool.	101
6.2	The objective of this game – to practice the flutter kick transporting a foam ball without touching it with a kickboard.	105
7.1	Learners' suggestions in TGA-CL join as a "puzzle" for developing values and common goals.	118
7.2	Tactical time-out on TGA-SE.	123

* All figures were originally created and provided by Ramón Feire.

Tables

2.1	Examples of different types of questioning in invasion games.	28
2.2	Sessions' plan summary.	30
3.1	Examples of different questions for net/wall games.	44
3.2	Badminton sessions' plan summary.	45
4.1	General actions and tactical-technical components of striking/fielding games.	59
4.2	Examples of different questions for striking/fielding games.	60
4.3	Common tactical-technical elements based on the level of complexity on striking/fielding games.	61
4.4	Progression of tactical-technical learning through four stages in DGSM.	62
4.5	Example of grading game-play rubric for softball.	69
5.1	Examples of different questions for target games.	75
5.2	Target games' progression of tactical-technical complexity based on Sheppard and Mandigo (2003).	76
5.3	Tactical questions and their possible answers.	81
5.4	Technical questions and their possible answers of the skill drill practice.	82
5.5	General questions and their possible answers for the final part of the session.	83
5.6	An example of a GPAI registration sheet.	87
6.1	Examples of different questions for individual games.	95
6.2	Guidelines to master the seven basic swimming skills.	98
6.3	Specific motion patterns for each swimming style.	99
6.4	Crosstab proposed by Grosse (2005) to help coaches/teachers to effectively design comprehensive assessment tools for individual games/sports.	107

6.5	An emergency performance checklist based on Fleischhackl et al. (2009) applied in different simulated scenarios.	108
7.1	Tools for verifying hybrid GCA implementation.	121
7.2	A typical day during pre-season.	124
7.3	A typical day during formal competition.	125

Series editor foreword

Learning about different pedagogical approaches is covered in many teacher and coach education courses around the world. What has been lacking for many coaches, teachers and pre-service teachers has been a guidebook or the reader's notes. Like Shakespeare, research is often, but not always, written in a language that distances itself from the end user. The ideas are fantastic, the words mesmerizing, but the desire to make them sound fantastic comes at a cost (and is often dressed up in big words). It's no coincidence that Albert Einstein defined genius as "making complex ideas simple and not simple ideas complex." The desire to use bigger words often distances the reader from the idea. I have, all too often, put a book or a paper to one side because I simply can't engage with the ideas because of the writing.

The Game-Centred Approach to Sport Literacy, in contrast, is the reader notes for Game-Centred Approaches (GCAs). The authors have taken well-established ideas – ones that have baffled many a novice user – and provided much-needed help. They haven't dumbed it down. This isn't "an idiot's guide." Instead it is a careful and thorough consideration of both the what and the how of GCAs. In each chapter they help the reader consider the modification process across a number of contexts and pedagogical models. They provide example sessions and ideas and guidance for assessment. In short, they do something that is much needed, that is, a praxis guided to GCAs. I suspect that this is a book I'll be using with my students on a regular basis.

Ash Casey
5 May 2020

1 Building the Game-Centred Approach

A historical overview, implementation and transference

Why is it important to promote sports and physical activities?

Our world's constant evolution and the challenges associated with globalization are present in educational, personal and professional spheres. Nowadays, information and communication technology (ICT) occupies a central place in our lives. These technologies are designed and updated to make our lives easier, although paradoxically, they have led humans to increase sedentary behaviours to an extent that it is considered one of the diseases of the 21st century (Arocha-Rudolfo, 2019). The increase in inactivity has seen a decline of physical activity levels among school-age children and adolescents around the world (Farooq et al., 2020).

The World Health Organization (WHO, 2010) published a comprehensive guideline to help individuals reach the minimum levels of physical activity needed to achieve the associated health benefits:

1 children and young people (5–17 years) should accumulate at least 60 minutes of moderate to vigorous physical activity daily;
2 adults (18–64 years) should accumulate at least 150 minutes of moderate physical activity weekly; and
3 elderly people (more than 65 years) should perform at least 150 minutes of moderate physical activity weekly.

The promotion of sport and physical activity among youngsters should be encouraged not only in schools, where physical education is the only subject that involves education through the physical, but also in extracurricular activities. A central issue, however, is how to develop effective sport programmes that help young people learn the basic tactical-technical elements whilst simultaneously promoting sport engagement. The way sports are taught (i.e., sport pedagogy) has been shown to be a key element in increasing students' motivation to practice and maintain sporting activity into adulthood (Martin, 2020), which connects with the concept of physical literacy proposed by Whitehead which implies the "motivation, confidence, physical competence, knowledge and understanding to maintain activity throughout the life course" (2010, pp. 11–12).

An historical overview: the traditional approach of teaching sports/games

Traditionally, sports teaching/coaching has been focused on the technical development of skills based on decontextualized and repetitive drill-based methods (Standing & Maulder, 2019). Although these methods can be termed differently depending on the context (e.g., skill-drill-game, direct instruction), the concept of "coach-centred" approach will be used throughout this book.

The coach-centred approach was defined by Pill (2018, p. 1) as a traditional style of coaching (or teaching), which is "directive, commanding and prescriptive coaching, emphasizing conformity and transmission of information for reproduction." In other words, players do what the instructor tells them to do, and consequently, this approach disempowers players and places instructors at the axis of the teaching-learning process. This approach is based on the belief that learning how to play games properly requires the player to reach a minimum level of competence in performing techniques that are thought to be fundamental to the game before they can play the game itself (Light, 2014a). According to Light (2014b), the teaching-learning process is focused on reducing skill mistakes and mechanically acquiring the correct technique, which is a combination of skills applied for a specific sport. The instructor is considered an expert, both in the sport content and in skills management, because they have to transfer the content and specific techniques using the most efficient and effective way. Although this traditional approach can be viewed slightly differently depending on the experience and expertise of the instructors, Kruzel (1985) proposed that the common factor in different traditional approaches is that athletes are always involved in a coach-directed learning style that provides a progression of activities, normally skill drills, to master certain techniques.

Bunker and Thorpe (1982) were critical of this approach. They considered that traditional methods of teaching sports and games had failed to consider the contextual nature and authenticity of games. Light (2014a) observed that the implementation of these methods both in educational and extracurricular contexts could promote selfishness, egotism, lack of empathy or compassion for teammates and failure to teach teamwork. In addition, a recent meta-analysis showed that the self-determination index (quantification of motivation) significantly decreased when traditional approaches were implemented (Sierra-Díaz, González-Víllora, Pastor-Vicedo, & López-Sánchez, 2019).

A change in the conception: the athlete/student-centred perspective

Pill (2018, p. 1) defines an athlete-centred coaching approach as "a style of coaching that promotes athlete learning through athlete ownership, responsibility, initiative and awareness, guided by the coach." Over the years, specific terms have been used to designate these pedagogical methodologies focused on the players, which constitute solid action plans (Metzler, 2017) and can be used both in physical education and sport contexts: *curriculum models* (Thorpe & Bunker, 1986; Jewett, Bain, & Ennis, 1995), *instructional models* (Metzler, 2005) or *pedagogical models* (Haerens, Kirk, Cardon, & De Bourdeaudhuij, 2011). Throughout this book, following the recommendation of Haerens et al. (2011), the term *pedagogical models* will be used because it reinforces the idea that models can be applied beyond the educational context in extracurricular sport activities or in leisure settings.

Pedagogical models are a consolidated alternative to replace traditional practice, influenced by similar pedagogical tenets based on constructivism. Baker (2016) indicated that *pedagogical models* can be adapted to different contexts, offering inclusive, relevant and contextualized physical activity practices, including consolidated learner-centred frameworks. The inclusion of all players is a pre-requisite for developing physically literate players (Whitehead, 2010).

Historically, the first model created as a response to the exclusive focus on techniques, as well as the lack of motivation among less-skilled players, was *Teaching Games for Understanding* (TGfU; Bunker & Thorpe, 1982). After the publication of the handbook *Rethinking games teaching* (Thorpe, Bunker, & Almond, 1986), the model spread around the world, but it also was adapted to each particular cultural context (Sánchez-Gómez et al., 2014). This led to the creation of new models based originally on the TGfU, such as the *Tactical Games Model* in the United States (Mitchell, Oslin, & Griffin, 2003) or *Game Sense* in Australia (den Duyn, 1997). As a result of this emergence, a new term to encompass all those which shared similar features was needed (Forrest, 2014): the Game-Centred Approach (GCA). Figure 1.1 encourages all readers to make the shift from a traditional approach to player-centred pedagogies. This book aims to address this important goal.

Figure 1.1 Shift from traditional approach to athlete/student-centred pedagogies.

The development of the Game-Centred Approach (GCA)

The GCA (Oslin & Mitchell, 2006) is an umbrella term for pedagogical approaches and models with the game and reflections on game play as the central elements for learning (Forrest, 2014). This approach is also referred as the *Game-Based Approach* (Kinnerk, Harvey, MacDonncha, & Lyons, 2018; Light & Mooney, 2014) to avoid confusion with the abbreviation and concept of the Singaporean *games concept approach*.

According to Light and Mooney (2014), the origin of this concept can be traced back even before the emergence of TGfU to the works of Wade (1967) and Mahlo (1974). However, Bunker and Thorpe's proposal (1982, 1986), and its curricular adaptations around the world, consolidated the need to integrate them all under the umbrella term *GCA* (Forrest, 2014).

Regarding the nature of GCAs, Harvey, Cushion and Sammon (2015) highlighted the implementation of modified games oriented to the development of a specific technique alongside tactical problems as the most important common feature of this approach. Comparatively, Harvey, Cope and Jones (2016) also emphasized the use of questioning strategies to help participants build their own knowledge to reflect the best strategy and technique against a real tactical game problem. Considering both features, Light (2013) stressed that the first step in developing critical thinking is to allow athletes to discover independently the solution to tactical problems

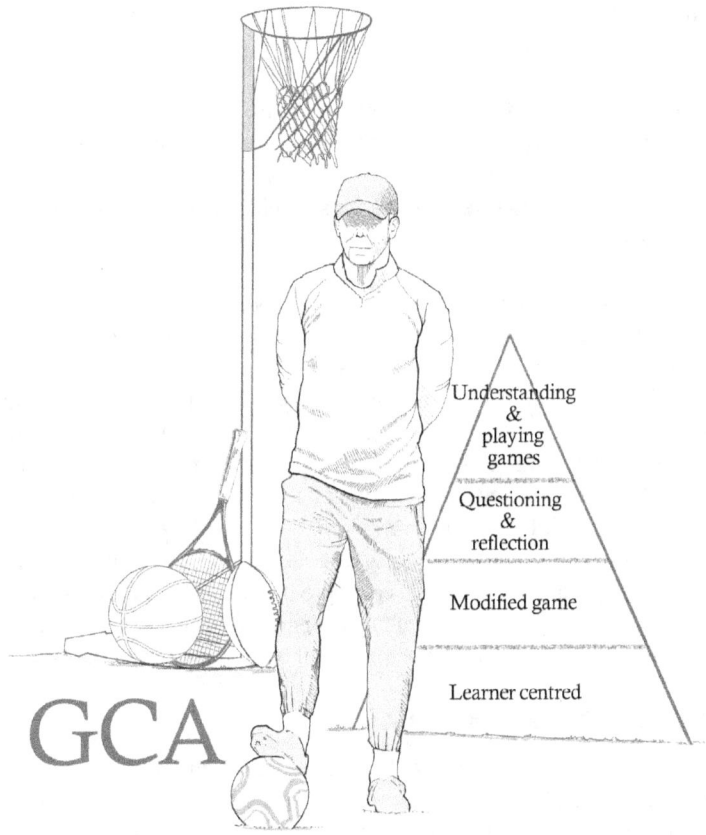

Figure 1.2 Main features of GCAs.

continually presented in a game-form situation. The second step is to invite athletes to reflect on important elements occurring in the game by using questioning strategies. Figure 1.2 summarizes the main features of GCAs.

The game as the central element of GCAs

Games are, unquestionably, the main element in this approach. However, as Mitchell, Oslin and Griffin (2013) warned, they should be adapted to fit the players' needs. For this reason, the term *modified games* is used to emphasize a comprehensive tactical/technical development simplifying the features of real sports, such as number of players, time or court length (Almond, 2015). Modified games have been divided taking into account two basic concepts (Mitchell et al., 2013):

- **Representation of games:** maintains the essence of the real game, but tactical complexity is adapted to the characteristics of the players (e.g., 3x3 basketball game).
- **Exaggeration of games:** emphasizes specific elements of the real sport (i.e., a tactical principle or technique).

Regarding competitive team sports, especially soccer, the term *small-sided (and conditioned) games* (SSCGs) is widely used (Clemente, 2016). SSCGs involve the reduction of the playing field or the number of players together with basic rules, such as the role of the players or the rules of the game, to fit their needs (Robles, Fernández-Espínola, & Fuentes-Guerra, 2019). Scientific literature has shown that SSCGs are a great alternative to traditional drills because they help individuals learn techniques and develop decision-making skills (Davids, Araújo, Correia, & Vilar, 2013). In addition, according to Sánchez-Sánchez, García, Asián-Clemente, Nakamura, Ramírez-Campillo (2019), SSCGs can reproduce the demands of real games, emphasizing important tactical-technical elements. Each adaptation can produce different results. Several examples will be presented later.

Games classification and transference

Based on the ideas of Ellis (1983), later reorganized by Almond (1986), sports were grouped in five categories which share similar structure and internal logic based on the same tactical features: target (e.g., bowling), fielding/run score (e.g., baseball), net/wall (e.g., badminton) and invasion games (e.g., handball). The following chapters exhaustively describe each game category, including individual games (e.g., athletics), and practically propose an example of how to implement different GCA models.

Similarities among games in the same category allow knowledge transference from one game to another (Casey & MacPhail, 2018) because they share the same tactical principles.

The different GCAs

Teaching Games for Understanding (TGfU)

The official term *Teaching Games for Understanding* (TGfU) was used by Bunker and Thorpe in 1982, although their model was based on the work of several teachers and academics. TGfU was the first model that changed the concept of decontextualized practice observed at schools (Webb & Pearson, 2012). Briefly, the focus of the model is to place the learner in a game situation where tactics, decision-making and problem-solving are non-negotiable features, although skill drills are also used to correct any habit or reinforce any skill.

This model was the first one to change the awareness of sport literacy, both in educational and extracurricular contexts. It was the first change that encouraged critical thinking which hinged on contextualized game forms and inquiry-based and reflective strategies (Culpan & Galvan, 2012). Originally, Bunker and Thorpe (1982) proposed a circular structure of six moments that should be present in every session: game, game appreciation, tactical awareness, making appropriate decision, skill execution and performance. In essence, the game practice is placed in the centre of the teaching-learning process (Kirk & MacPhail, 2002).

After Bunker and Thorpe's (1982) first publication, and the book *Rethinking Games Teaching* (Thorpe et al., 1986), this model spread around the world. However, as Kirk (2017) highlighted, a model should not be considered a blueprint. For that reason, adaptations and restructuring of the original TGfU were made around the world, such as in the United States (Werner, 1989; Mitchell, 1996), Australia (Kirk, 1989) and Spain (Devís-Devís & Peiró, 1992), which led to the emergence of similar, and now consolidated, models.

Chapter 5 (p. 72) includes a practical example of how to apply TGfU in the category of target games. Readers are invited to adapt the practical proposal to other categories of games.

The Tactical Games Approach (TGA)

The *Tactical Games Approach* (TGA; Griffin, Mitchell, and Oslin, 1997) is a version of the TGfU model adapted to the American context. Mitchell et al. (2013) believed that traditional games teaching in schools had done little to educate students on game playing. For that reason, they proposed a tactical approach to promote interest, understanding and the ability to play games. These authors suggested that tactical problems in each game category can be divided in different levels of tactical complexity, and specific sports' tactical problems can also be taught following a tactical progression.

Since its inclusion in games teaching and development, tactical games has been considered one of the prominent GCAs (Oslin & Mitchell, 2006), and several books have been written since its development (Griffin et al., 1997; Mitchell et al., 2003, 2006, 2013). The main goal of this GCA is to create tactically and technically smart players who have to select the best strategy and employ the required skill to overcome tactical problems in games.

Griffin et al. (1997) proposed a simplified four-stage framework to implement the TGA, which focuses on the essential lesson components of the TGfU: first, athletes play a modified game that highlights a particular tactical problem, which becomes the instructional focus. Second, questions are designed to develop tactical awareness (i.e., understanding of what to do to solve a problem). Third, situated practices guide the learner to practice essential skills or movements to solve tactical problems presented by the initial game or game form. Fourth, the final game provides students with the opportunity to use their knowledge in a real setting (Mitchell et al., 2003). Chapter 2 (p. 23) presents a practical application of the TGA in soccer, and Chapter 7 (p. 112) provides an example of how to hybridize this model with sport education.

Game Sense (GS)

Thorpe visited Australia to work with coaches and the Australian Sports Commission to develop an adaptation of the TGfU focused on extracurricular contexts. This version received the name of *Game Sense* (GS; den Duyn, 1997; Light, 2013), and it is mainly focused on the coaching context. In physical education, GS is used to introduce students how to play a game from a wide range of games/sport, whereas when applied to coaching, GS is used to fit into a season of competition (Light, 2013). The focus in GS is on learning, understood as a social process in which learners are "inseparably intertwined" (Light, 2013, p. 33).

The design of the learning process needs to suit the desired learning outcomes and the knowledge, abilities and interests of the players and provide for modifications to make it more/less challenging for players (Light, 2013). In GS, skills are learnt "*in* and *through* (modified) games" (Light, 2013, p. 51). According to Mandigo, Butler, and Hopper (2007), GS is based upon individuals' abilities to develop sport and physical ability skills through game-centred activities designed to improve learners' decision-making, thinking and problem-solving skills and physical performance in an interactive environment. Chapter 3 (p. 40) presents a practical application of badminton through GS.

Play Practice (PP)

There are some approaches that have been developed during the emergence of TGfU, which are not directly adapted from it. *Play Practice*

Building the Game-Centred Approach 9

(PP; Launder, 2001) was originally created in extracurricular contexts in Australia. Depending on the game category, PP is structured in different moments. The session must start with a simplified game involving specific skills or techniques. Thereafter the instructor is in charge of analyzing the progression of the players and thereby proposes new challenges or games. Chapter 6 (p. 92) presents a practical application of this model in swimming.

Tactical-Decision Learning Model (T-DLM)

Like PP, the French *Tactical-Decision Learning Model* (T-DLM; Gréhaigne, Richard, & Griffin, 2005) is not directly created from TGfU. The main objective of T-DLM is to foster the students' exploration of game play as well as the consolidation of adequate responses inside SSCGs. To reach this goal, the model has a spiral structure. It starts with simple SSCGs, and the tactical complexity increases gradually. At the end of each game, a debate of ideas, guided by the instructor, is carried out, reinforcing those important elements previously experienced during the game. After the debate, players may perceive the emergence of different key elements of the game, which has to be positively related to the following action proposal.

Developmental Games Stage Model (DGSM)

The *Developmental Games Stage Model* (DGSM; Rink, 2002), also called the *skill development approach* (Araújo et al., 2017), is based on the same foundation as the rest of the GCAs (Graca & Mesquita, 2015): the learning process of a game should enhance satisfaction and tactical-technical development in a progressive learning sequence (Belka, 2004). The DGSM is rooted in two basic notions: the modification of the games has to steer the adaptation and progression of the practice condition, and the level of difficulty of the games has to take into account the participants' characteristics as well as their previous experience (Rink, 2002); a later publication stresses the importance of developing and promoting active lifestyles (Rink, 2008).

DGSM is based on three basic principles (i.e., progression or extension, performance or refinement and application or assessment Mesquita & Graça, 2009). The principle of progression emphasizes the importance of progressively structuring the content through the following four stages (Rink, 2002): (1) single skills, (2) combining skills, (3) beginning offensive and defensive play and (4) regulation play. The principle of refinement is a methodological approach that reinforces the idea that the development of skills and strategies is a determinant factor in the learning process. Finally, the principle of application emphasizes the objective of each game as well as the role of each participant including their personal commitment and autonomy.

10 Building the Game-Centred Approach

This model is practically explained in Chapter 4 (p. 58). Readers are invited to consider its adaptation to their specific context.

Non-linear pedagogy and constraints-led approach

Non-linear pedagogy involves manipulating key task constraints to facilitate the emergence of functional movement patterns and decision-making behaviours. Additionally, instructors must understand the interacting constraints on each individual learner and how to manipulate key task constraints to facilitate the emergence of functional movement repertoires. According to Chow et al. (2006), manipulation of constraints can lead to the production of successful motor patterns, decision-making behaviour and intentions that guide the achievement of task goals.

There are three different kinds of constraints (Chow et al., 2007):

- **Performer constraints:** structural and functional characteristics of an individual, both physical attributes (e.g., height, weight and body composition) and functional characteristics (e.g., synapses in the brain, motivations, emotions and cognition).
- **Environmental constraints:** those found in the context (e.g., light, temperature or altitude) and social constrains (e.g., peer groups, social norms or cultural expectations).
- **Task constraints:** rules, equipment, playing areas, goals or number of players.

Other GCAs

Readers should take into account that there are a wide range of models which share the same features of the GCA, but they have not been widely described before (e.g., Game Insight Approach, Games Concept Approach or the Invasion Games Competence Model), or other emergent proposals such as the Contextualized Sport Alphabetization Model (CSAM) in Spain (González-Víllora Sierra-Díaz, Pastor-Vicedo, & Contreras-Jordán 2019).

Shared features of GCAs

GCAs are based on the premise that the learning experiences provided can contribute to the social, moral and personal development. This will occur through the main elements of this approach, which can be summarized as follows:

1 Focus on the game instead of decontextualized techniques or skills through modified games or game-like activities (Light, 2013) – GCAs

use both techniques and tactics to develop understanding, and games are modified and adapted to fit learners' demands.
2   Emphasis on questioning stimulates thinking and interaction (Wright & Forrest, 2007).
3   Dialogue, reflection and social interaction play important roles in developing understanding (Light, 2014b).

Despite the differences, these approaches can provide positive experiences that enhance learning and promote both the ability and the inclination to learn because they are "student-centred, inquiry-based approaches that emphasize learner reflection upon experience and social interaction" (Light, 2014a, p. 29).

Preparing students for GCAs

Mitchell et al. (2003) highlighted that a tactical approach requires that players engage in game play independently in small groups and provided several suggestions to prepare young learners to adapt to tactical games, which could be considered common for any GCA:

1   They must learn simple rules and routines that will help in the effective use of time (e.g., learners organize their own equipment and begin activity immediately).
2   They must respect other learners when playing small-sided games (e.g., do not interrupt when a ball enters into another court).
3   They develop sport behaviour (e.g., roles and responsibilities).

Pedagogical principles for shifting instructors' leadership styles

Based on Thorpe et al.'s (1986) work, Griffin, Butler and Sheppard (2018) described the following pedagogical principles for shifting instructors' leadership styles.

Instructor as a facilitator of learning

GCAs are based on shifting responsibility from instructors to learners. Within this approach, young learners gain a relevant role in their learning process. The instructor acts as facilitator setting problems, goals and/or boundaries that guide tasks (Griffin et al., 2018), and players search for solutions. As suggested by Griffin et al. (2018, p. 13): "in order for students to become good players, they need to become good problem solvers."

To support this shift of responsibility, instructors must create active learning practices, giving time to players to integrate their new role (Griffin et al., 2018). Effective learning reflection through questioning and/or inquiry-based strategies (Butler, 1997) is essential in GCAs. Instructors will promote learning through questions. They need to learn when to ask questions and when to provide answers (Griffin et al., 2018). In this sense, a key element of the planning process is the development of quality questions (Bunker & Thorpe, 1982; Griffin et al., 2018; Mitchell et al., 2013). Scientific literature on GCAs has emphasized the importance of elaborating and applying high-quality questions (Australian Sports Commission, 1997; Bunker & Thorpe, 1982; Griffin et al., 1997). However, Harvey and Light (2015) claimed that questioning can be difficult to implement during games. Griffin et al. proposed six types of questions and the game aspects they can cover (2018, p. 14):

1 Tactical or strategic awareness: "What do you . . .?"
2 Skill and movement execution: "How do you . . .?"
3 Time: "When is the best time to . . .?"
4 Space: "Where is/can . . .?"
5 Risk: "Which choice . . .?"
6 Rationale: "Why are you . . .?"

The practical chapters on this book will provide specific examples on how to adapt these questions to the different game categories. The questioning strategy should also take into consideration psychological factors. Pearson and Webb (2008) observed that attitude and intonation of the questions might increase students' positive attitude and autonomous motivation because they feel more self-confident in developing their own ideas.

Although several game-centred models do not indicate when to introduce questions (e.g., DGSM, PP), instructors should always consider their use to reinforce an idea, concept, tactical problem, skill or technique. In other words, pedagogical strategies of active reflection should be an integral part of the planning process of every GCA.

Gréhaigne et al. (2005) proposed the strategic debate of ideas. This enables players to share their opinions about specific elements of the game through the identification of opposing players' particular strengths and the strategies to cope with these strengths.

On the other hand, Whitmore (2009) proposed the goal, reality, options/obstacles and will/way forward (GROW) strategy to reinforce the key elements of the game. Harvey et al. (2016) proposed four steps to implement this technique:

1 establish the goal of the activity;
2 analyze the athlete's reality;

3 focus on the obstacles and its potential solution; and
4 establish an effective action plan for the game.

Tactical complexity

Tactical complexity involves the tactical concepts (e.g., progression to the goal) and movement concepts of games and the abilities and skills needed to implement these concepts (Howarth, Fisette, Sweeney, & Griffin, 2010). It determines the difficulty of the task that the learners are going to face.

Modifications (representation, exaggeration and adaptation)

Proponents of GCAs argue that if the game is shaped and modified, all players can have success and integrate meaningful learning (Griffin et al., 2018). These authors proposed that instructors should consider the pedagogical principle of modification through the following:

1 **Representation:** "do less to get more": the game can be streamlined, reducing the number of players but maintaining the main features of the game (e.g., 2x2 in futsal).
2 **Exaggeration:** some aspects of the play are emphasized to encourage particular tactical content (e.g., four goals for three players, in which the emphasis is on trying to score; Evangelio, Sierra-Díaz, González-Víllora, & Clemente, 2019).
3 **Adaptation:** once the player has been successful, the game is modified to make it more challenging (e.g., during a 3x3 game, all players have to dribble the basketball with the non-dominant hand).

More examples of the different modifications are presented throughout the book (practical chapters). These modifications help instructors streamline the sport (Griffin et al., 2018) to a simple game, tactics, strategies or movements. Griffin et al. (2018) highlighted five aspects of the game that can be exaggerated or adapted to focus on particular tactical problems:

1 **Rules:** to work on specific tactical and/or technical elements.
2 **Number of players:** using small-sided games or game forms (3x3 or 2x1) to slow the tempo and flow of the game, limiting its tactical complexity and simplifying the decision-making process.
3 **Playing area:** to help players focus on particular aspects of the game (e.g., move to open areas).
4 **Equipment:** adapted to help players feel safer, allowing for more successful executions of skills and movements.
5 **Scoring or modifying the goal:** to reinforce offensive or defensive practice.

Assessment of learning outcomes

Siedentop and Tannehill (2000) defined assessment as involving different tasks and settings where learners are given opportunities to "demonstrate their knowledge, skill, understanding and application of content in a context that allows continued learning and growth" (p. 179). Assessment should not be only the evaluation/measurement of the expected product. It should also help learners understand the process of learning and help instructors evaluate how well learners have met the learning outcomes set at the beginning.

Sport assessment traditionally relied on skill testing to measure motor skill development and performance. However, using skill tests in decontextualized assessment of motor skill performance is problematic. Hay (2006) suggested a shift from assessment *of* learning (summative assessments at the end) to assessment *for* learning (to inform and provide feedback to learners on their progress). Wiggins (2011) suggested that authentic assessment meet the following criteria:

- It should be truly representative of performance in the field.
- Both the physical and social contexts should be considered.
- Self-assessment plays a greater role than traditional testing.
- Learners are expected to present and defend their work publicly, meaning mastering the task.

Within this book, specific instruments will be presented.

GCAs and physical literacy

The concept of physical literacy

Following Whitehead (2010), the concept of physical literacy emerged from the decreasing importance of movement development in early childhood (concentrated on the development of language and social skills), the exacerbation of problems such as obesity and poor physical and mental health, and the critique of physical education neglecting those pupils who did not have outstanding ability. In Whitehead's words (2010, pp. 11–12), "physical literacy can be described as the motivation, confidence, physical competence, knowledge and understanding to maintain activity throughout the life course."

Research on invasion games through GCAs: attributes for a physically literate individual

A recent review conducted by Harvey and Jarrett (2014) showed a predominance of invasion games in the GCAs literature. The following section provides evidence on the positive findings and limitations of GCAs in invasion games and its repercussion on physical literacy. Dudley (2015) and SHAPE America (2014) suggest the following for a physical literacy player:

- **Demonstrates competence in motor skill and movement patterns:** Kinnerk et al. (2018), in a recent review in coaching contexts, suggested that there was limited evidence to support technical development from GCAs. In the same way, Harvey and Jarrett (2014) highlighted that there were equivocal results on skill development in comparative research (tactical treatment versus technical treatment group), but there is no evidence that technical skill development declined as a consequence of the use of GCAs (Kinnerk et al., 2018). Recent research has shown positive results on skill execution variables (Gouveia et al., 2019; Morales-Belando, Calderón, & Arias-Estero, 2018).
- **Knows the rules, principles, strategies and tactics related to movement and performance:** a recent review of GCAs in team sports showed positive results in decision-making and tactical awareness (Kinnerk et al., 2018). Research on GCAs has shown to be helpful for students' development of overall game performance (Morales-Belando et al., 2018), as well as tactical transference (Gouveia et al., 2019; Memmert & Harvey, 2010) and the development of declarative knowledge (Nathan & Haynes, 2013). Gray and Sproule (2011) showed better results in decision-making than a skill-focused group, and the perception of players' improvement was evident only in the game-based group.
- **Demonstrates the knowledge and skills to achieve and maintain a health-enhancing level of fitness and physical activity:** there is limited research on fitness and health provision via GCAs (Harvey & Jarrett, 2014; Kinnerk et al., 2018; Oslin & Mitchell, 2006). Some research has provided positive findings regarding opportunities to reach the recommended physical activity goals in physical education (Gouveia et al., 2019; Harvey, Song, Baek, & Van Der Mars, 2016). In comparative studies, moderate-to-vigorous physical activity (MVPA) was significantly higher in GCAs than in technique-focused approaches (Smith et al., 2015).
- **Exhibits personal and social behaviour and recognizes the value of physical activity for health, enjoyment, challenge, self-expression and/or social interaction:** recent reviews have shown the potential of GCAs to create enjoyable learning environments and promote learning in the affective domain (Harvey & Jarrett, 2014; Miller, 2015). A key strength of GCAs was that the coach adopted the role of facilitator, encouraging player empowerment and responsibility (Kinnerk et al., 2018). The coaches positively perceived the shifting of responsibility

(Llobet-Martí et al., 2018). From the players' perspective, they reported improved communication and teamwork (Harvey, 2009), self-determined motivation (Harvey, Gil-Arias, Smith, & Smith, 2017) or perceived competence and enjoyment (Gil-Arias, Claver, Práxedes, Villar, & Harvey, 2020).

Summary

This chapter provides an overview on how GCAs were developed and its main features (e.g., modified games, questioning). Finally, the link between GCAs and physical literacy is presented, which will serve to lay the foundations for the following chapters.

References

Almond, L. (1986). Reflecting on themes: a games classification. In R. D. Thorpe, D. J. Bunker, & L. Almond (Eds.), *Rethinking games teaching* (pp. 71–77). Loughborough: Department of Physical Education and Sports Sciences of the University of Loughborough.

Almond, L. (2015). Rethinking Teaching Games for Understanding. *Ágora for Physical Education and Sport, 17*(1), 15–25.

Araújo, R., Hastie, P. A., Pereira, C., & Mesquita, I. (2017). The evolution of student-coach's pedagogical content knowledge in a combined use of Sport Education and the Step-Game-Approach model. *Physical Education & Sport Pedagogy, 22*(5), 518–535. https://doi.org/10.1080/17408989.2017.1294668

Arocha-Rudolfo, J. I. (2019). Sedentarism, a disease from XXI century. *Clínica e Investigación en Arteriosclerosis, 31*(5), 233–240. https://doi.org/10.1016/j.arteri.2019.04.004

Australian Sports Commission. (1997). *Game Sense. Developing thinking players.* Belconnen, Australian Capital Territory: Australian Sports Commission.

Baker, K. (2016). Models-based practice: learning from and questioning the existing Canadian physical education literature. *Canadian Journal for New Scholars in Education, 7*(2), 47–58.

Belka, D. E. (2004). Combining and sequencing games skills. *Journal of Physical Education, Recreation & Dance, 75*(4), 23–27. https://doi.org/10.1080/07303084.2004.10609263

Bunker, D. J., & Thorpe, R. D. (1982). A model for the teaching of games in secondary schools. *Bulletin of Physical Education, 18*(1), 5–8.

Butler, R. (1997). Stories and experiments in social inquiry. *Organization Studies, 18*(6), 927–948. https://doi.org/10.1177/017084069701800602

Casey, A., & MacPhail, A. (2018). Adopting a models-based approach to teaching physical education. *Physical Education & Sport Pedagogy, 23*(3), 294–310. https://doi.org/10.1080/17408989.2018.1429588

Chow, J. Y., Davids, K., Button, C., Shuttleworth, R., Renshaw, I., & Araújo, D. (2006). Nonlinear pedagogy: a constraints-led framework for understanding emergence of game play and movement skills. *Nonlinear Dynamics, Psychology, and Life Sciences, 10*(1), 71–103.

Chow, J. Y., Davids, K., Button, C., Shuttleworth, R., Renshaw, I., & Araújo, D. (2007). The role of nonlinear pedagogy in physical education. *Review of Educational Research, 77*(3), 251–278. https://doi.org/10.3102/003465430305615

Clemente, F. M. (2016). *Small-Sided and Conditioned Games in soccer training: the science and practical applications*. Berlin, Germany: Springer.

Culpan, I., & Galvan, H. (2012). Physical education in New Zealand: a sociocritical and bi-cultural positioning. *Journal of Physical Education and Health, 1*(1), 31–42.

Davids, K., Araújo, D., Correia, V., & Vilar, L. (2013). How Small-Sided and Conditioned Games enhance acquisition of movement and decision-making skills. *Exercise and Sport Sciences Reviews, 41*(3), 154–161. https://doi.org/10.1097/JES.0b013e318292f3ec

den Duyn, N. (1997). *Game Sense: developing thinking players*. Canberra: Australian Sports Commission.

Devís-Devís, J., & Peiró, C. (1992). *Nuevas perspectivas curriculares en Educación Física: la salud y los juegos modificados* [Proposed English translation: *New curricular perspectives in physical education: health and modified games*]. Barcelona, Spain: Inde Editorial.

Dudley, D. A. (2015). A conceptual model of observed physical literacy. *The Physical Educator, 72*(5), 236–260. https://doi.org/10.18666/TPE-2015-V72-I5-6020

Ellis, M. (1983). Similarities and differences in games: a system for classification. Conference paper presented at *International Association for Physical Education in Higher Education (AIESEP) Conference*. Rome, Italy.

Evangelio, C., Sierra-Díaz, M. J., González-Víllora, S., & Clemente, F. M. (2019). 'Four goals for three players': using 3 vs. 3 Small-Sided Games at school. *Human Movement, 20*(2), 68–78. https://doi.org/10.5114/hm.2019.85096

Farooq, A., Martin, A., Janssen, X., Wilson, M. G., Gibson, A. M., Hughes, A., & Reilly, J. J. (2020). Longitudinal changes in moderate-to-vigorous-intensity physical activity in children and adolescents: a systematic review and meta-analysis. *Obesity Reviews, 21*(1), 1–15. https://doi.org/10.1111/obr.12953

Forrest, G. (2014). Questions and answers: understanding the connection between questioning and knowledge in Game-Centred Approaches. In R. Light, J. Quay, S. Harvey, & A. Mooney (Eds.), *Contemporary developments in games teaching* (pp. 167–177). Abingdon, Oxford: Routledge.

Gil-Arias, A., Claver, F., Práxedes, A., Villar, F. D., & Harvey, S. (2020). Autonomy support, motivational climate, enjoyment and perceived competence in physical education: impact of a hybrid Teaching Games for Understanding/Sport Education unit. *European Physical Education Review, 26*(1), 36–53. https://doi.org/10.1177/1356336X18816997

González-Víllora, S., Sierra-Díaz, M. J., Pastor-Vicedo, J. C., & Contreras-Jordán, O. R. (2019). The way to increase the motor and sport competence among children: the Contextualized Sport Alphabetization Model. *Frontiers in Physiology*, *10*, 569. https://doi.org/10.3389/fphys.2019.00569

Gouveia, É. R., Gouveia, B. R., Marques, A., Kliegel, M., Rodrigues, A. J., Prudente, J., . . . Ihle, A. (2019). The effectiveness of a Tactical Games Approach in the teaching of invasion games. *Journal of Physical Education and Sport*, *19*, 962–970.

Graça, A. & Mesquita, I. (2015). Modelos e conceçôes de ensino dos jogos desportivos [Proposed English translation: *Models and concepts for teaching sports games*]. In F. Tavares (Ed.), Jogos Desportivos Colectivos Ensinar a Jogar (pp. 9–54) [Proposed English translation: *Collective sports games. Teach to play*]. Portugal: Editora.

Gray, S., & Sproule, J. (2011). Developing pupils' performance in team invasion games. *Physical Education & Sport Pedagogy*, *16*(1), 15–32. https://doi.org/10.1080/17408980903535792

Gréhaigne, J. F., Richard, J.-F., & Griffin, L. (2005). *Teaching and learning team sports and games*. New York: Routledge-Falmer.

Griffin, L., Butler, J., & Sheppard, J. (2018). Athlete-centred coaching: extending the possibilities of a holistic and process-oriented model to athlete development. In S. Pill (Ed.), *Perspectives on athlete-centred coaching* (pp. 9–23). Abingdon, Oxford: Routledge.

Griffin, L., Mitchell, S., & Oslin, J. (1997). *Teaching sport concepts and skills: a tactical games approach*. Champaign, IL: Human Kinetics.

Haerens, L., Kirk, D., Cardon, G., & De Bourdeaudhuij, I. (2011) Toward the development of a pedagogical model for Health-based Physical Education. *Quest*, *63*(3), 321–338. https://doi.org/10.1080/00336297.2011.10483684

Harvey, S. (2009). A study of interscholastic soccer players' perceptions of learning with Game Sense. *Asian Journal of Exercise & Sports Science*, *6*(1), 1–10.

Harvey, S., Cope, E., & Jones, R. (2016). Developing questioning in Game-Centered Approaches. *Journal of Physical Education, Recreation & Dance*, *87*(3), 28–35. https://doi.org/10.1080/07303084.2015.1131212

Harvey, S., Cushion, C., & Sammon, P. (2015). Dilemmas faced by pre-service teachers when learning about and implementing a Game-Centred Approach. *European Physical Education Review*, *21*(2), 238–256. https://doi.org/10.1177/1356336X14560773

Harvey, S., Gil-Arias, A., Smith, M. L., & Smith, L. R. (2017). Middle and elementary school students' changes in self-determined motivation in a basketball unit taught using the Tactical Games Model. *Journal of Human Kinetics*, *59*(1), 39–53. https://doi.org/10.1515/hukin-2017-0146

Harvey, S., & Jarrett, K. (2014). A review of the Game-Centred Approaches to teaching and coaching literature since 2006. *Physical Education & Sport Pedagogy*, *19*(3), 278–300. https://doi.org/10.1080/17408989.2012.754005

Harvey, S., & Light, R. L. (2015). Questioning for learning in Game-Based Approaches to teaching and coaching. *Asia-Pacific Journal of Health, Sport and Physical Education*, *6*(2), 175–190. doi:10.1080/18377122.2015.1051268

Harvey, S., Song, Y., Baek, J. H., & Van Der Mars, H. (2016). Two sides of the same coin: student physical activity levels during a game-centred soccer unit. *European Physical Education Review*, *22*(4), 411–429. https://doi.org/10.1177/1356336X15614783

Hay, P. J. (2006). Assessment for learning in physical education. In D. Kirk, D. Macdonald, & M. O'Sullivan (Eds.), *The handbook of physical education* (pp. 312–326). Thousand Oaks, United States: SAGE Publications Ltd.

Howarth, K., Fisette, J., Sweeney, S., & Griffin, L. (2010). Unpacking tactical problems in invasion games: Integrating movement concepts into games education. In J. Butler, & L. Griffin (Eds.), *More Teaching Games for Understanding: moving globally* (pp. 245–256). Champaign, IL: Human Kinetics.

Jewett, A. E., Bain, L. L., & Ennis, C. D. (1995). *The curriculum process in physical education*. Dubuque, IA: Brown & Benchmark.

Kinnerk, P., Harvey, S., MacDonncha, C., & Lyons, M. (2018). A review of the Game-Based Approaches to coaching literature in competitive team sport settings. *Quest*, *70*(4), 401–418. https://doi.org/10.1080/00336297.2018.1439390

Kirk, D. (1989). Teaching Games for Understanding: an innovation in the games curriculum. *The Australian Council for Health, Physical Education and Recreation National Journal*, *126*(1), 25–27.

Kirk, D. (2017). Teaching games in physical education: towards a pedagogical model. *Revista Portuguesa de Ciências do Desporto*, *17*(S1.A), 17–26. https://doi.org/10.5628/rpcd.17.S1A.17

Kirk, D., & MacPhail, A. (2002). Teaching Games for Understanding and situated learning: rethinking the Bunker-Thorpe model. *Journal of teaching in Physical Education*, *21*(2), https://doi.org/177-192. 10.1123/jtpe.21.2.177

Kruzel, J. (1985). What's wrong with the traditional approach? *Washington Quarterly*, *8*(2), 121–132. https://doi.org/10.1080/01636608509450274

Launder, A. G. (2001). *Play practice: the games approach to teaching and coaching sports*. Champaign, IL: Human Kinetics.

Light, R. (2013). *Game sense. Pedagogy for performance, participation and enjoyment*. Abingdon, Oxford: Routledge.

Light, R. (2014a). Positive pedagogy for physical education and sport. Game Sense as an example. In R. Light, J. Quay, S. Harvey, & A. Mooney (Eds.), *Contemporary developments in games teaching* (pp. 29–42). Abingdon, Oxford: Routledge.

Light, R. (2014b). Learner-centred pedagogy for swim coaching: a complex learning theory-informed approach. *Asia-Pacific Journal of Health, Sport and Physical Education*, *5*(2), 167–180. https://doi.org/10.1080/18377122.2014.906056

Light, R., & Mooney, A. (2014). Introduction. In R. Light, J. Quay, S. Harvey, & A. Mooney (Eds.), *Contemporary developments in games teaching* (pp. 1–12). Abingdon, Oxford: Routledge.

Llobet-Martí, B., López-Ros, V., & Vila, I. (2018). The analysis of interactivity in a teaching and learning sequence of rugby: the transfer of control and learning responsibility. *Physical Education & Sport Pedagogy*, *23*(1), 84–102. https://doi.org/10.1080/17408989.2017.1341472

Mahlo, F. (1974). *Acte tactique en jeu* [Proposed English translation: *Tactical action in play*]. Paris, France: Vigot.

Mandigo, J., Butler, J., & Hopper, T. (2007). What is Teaching Games for Understanding? A Canadian perspective. *Physical and Health Education Journal*, *73*(2), 14–20.

Martin, N. J. (2020). Fostering motivation: understanding the role coaches play in youth sport. *Strategies, 33*(1), 20–27. https://doi.org/10.1080/08924562.2019.1680328

Memmert, D., & Harvey, S. (2010). Identification of non-specific tactical tasks in invasion games. *Physical Education & Sport Pedagogy, 15*(3), 287–305. https://doi.org/10.1080/17408980903273121

Mesquita, I., & Graça, A. (2009). Modelos instrucionais no ensino do desporto [Proposed English translation: Instructional Models for the teaching of sports]. *Pedagogia do Desporto,* 39–68.

Metzler, M. (2005). *Instructional models for physical education* (2nd ed.). New York: Routledge-Falmer.

Metzler, M. (2017). *Instructional models for physical education* (3rd ed.). New York: Routledge-Falmer.

Miller, A. (2015). Games Centered Approaches in teaching children & adolescents: Systematic review of associated student outcomes. *Journal of Teaching in Physical Education, 34*(1), 36–58. https://doi.org/10.1123/jtpe.2013-0155

Mitchell, S. A. (1996). Improving invasion game performance. *Journal of Physical Education, Recreation & Dance, 67*(2), 30–33. https://doi.org/10.1080/07303084.1996.10607197

Mitchell, S. A., Oslin, J. L., & Griffin, L. L. (2003). *Sport foundations for elementary physical education: a Tactical Games Approach*. Champaign, IL: Human Kinetics.

Mitchell, S. A., Oslin, J. L., & Griffin, L. L. (2006). *Teaching sport concepts and skills. A Tactical Games Approach*. Champaign, IL: Human Kinetics.

Mitchell, S. A., Oslin, J. L., & Griffin, L. L. (2013). *Teaching sport concepts and skills: a Tactical Games Approach for ages 7 to 18*. Champaign, IL: Human Kinetics.

Morales-Belando, M. T., Calderón, A., & Arias-Estero, J. L. (2018). Improvement in game performance and adherence after an aligned TGfU floorball unit in physical education. *Physical Education & Sport Pedagogy, 23*(6), 657–671. https://doi.org/10.1080/17408989.2018.1530747

Nathan, S., & Haynes, J. (2013). A move to an innovative games teaching model: Style E Tactical (SET). *Asia-Pacific Journal of Health, Sport and Physical Education, 4*(3), 287–302. https://doi.org/10.1080/18377122.2013.836769

Oslin, J., & Mitchell, S. (2006). Game-Centered Approaches to teaching physical education. In D. Kirk, D. Macdonald, & M. O'Sullivan (Eds.), *The handbook of physical education* (pp. 627–651). Thousand Oaks, United States: SAGE Publications Ltd.

Pearson, P. J., & Webb, P. (2008). Developing effective questioning in Teaching Games for Understanding (TGfU). Conference paper presented at *First Asia Pacific Sport in Education Conference*. Adelaide, Australia.

Pill, S. (2018). *Perspectives on athlete-centred coaching*. Abingdon, Oxford: Routledge.

Rink, J. E. (2002). *Teaching physical education for learning* (8th ed.). New York, United States of America: McGraw-Hill Education.

Rink, J. E. (2008). *Designing the physical education curriculum: Promoting active lifestyles*. New York, United States of America: McGraw-Hill Education.

Robles, M. T., Fernández-Espínola, C., & Fuentes-Guerra, F. J. (2019). Small games as a teaching methodology in football. *Revista Iberoamericana de Ciencias de la Actividad Física y el Deporte*, 8(1), 83–96.

Sánchez-Gómez, R., Devís-Devís, J., & Navarro-Adelantado, V. (2014). The Teaching Games for Understanding model in international and Spanish context: an historical perspective. *Ágora para la Educación Física y el Deporte*, 16(3), 197–213.

Sánchez-Sánchez, J., García, M. S., Asián-Clemente, J. A., Nakamura, F. Y., & Ramírez-Campillo, R. (2019). Effects of the directionality and the order of presentation within the session on the physical demands of small-sided games in youth soccer. *Asian Journal of Sports Medicine*, 10(2), 1–8. https://doi.org/10.5812/asjsm.87781

SHAPE America. (2014). *Grade-levels outcomes for K-12 Physical Education*. Reston: Human Kinetics and SHAPE America Press.

Siedentop, D., & Tannehill, D. (2000). *Developing teaching skills in physical education* (4th ed.). New York: McGraw-Hill.

Sierra-Díaz, M. J., González-Víllora, S., Pastor-Vicedo, J. C., & López-Sánchez, G. F. (2019). Can we motivate students to practice physical activities and sports through models-based practice? A systematic review and meta-analysis of psychosocial factors related to Physical Education. *Frontiers in Psychology*, 10, 2115 https://doi.org/10.3389/fpsyg.2019.02115

Smith, L., Harvey, S., Savory, L., Fairclough, S., Kozub, S., & Kerr, C. (2015). Physical activity levels and motivational responses of boys and girls: a comparison of direct instruction and Tactical Games Models of games teaching in physical education. *European Physical Education Review*, 21(1), 93–113. https://doi.org/10.1177/1356336X14555293

Standing, R., & Maulder, P. (2019). The effectiveness of progressive and traditional coaching strategies to improve sprint and jump performance across varying levels of maturation within a general youth population. *Sports*, 7(8), 186–206. https://doi.org/10.3390/sports7080186

Thorpe, R. D., & Bunker, D. J. (1986). The curriculum model. In R. D. Thorpe, D. J. Bunker, & L. Almond (Eds.), *Rethinking games teaching* (pp. 7–10). Loughborough, United Kingdom: Department of Physical Education and Sports Sciences; University of Loughborough.

Thorpe, R. D., Bunker, D. J., & Almond, L. (1986). *Rethinking games teaching*. United Kingdom: Department of Physical Education and Sports Sciences; Loughborough: University of Loughborough.

Wade, A. F. A. (1967). *The F.A. Guide to training and coaching*. London: The Football Association.

Webb, P. I., & Pearson, P. J. (2012). Creative unit and lesson planning through a thematic/integrated approach to Teaching Games for Understanding (TGfU). *New Zealand Physical Educator*, 45(3), 17–22.

Werner, E. E. (1989). Teaching games: a tactical perspective. *Journal of Physical Education, Recreation & Dance*, 60(3), 97–101.

Whitehead, M. (2010). *Physical literacy throughout the lifecourse*. Abingdon, Oxford: Routledge.

Whitmore, J. (2009). *Coaching for performance: GROWing human potential and purpose. The principles and practice of coaching and leadership* (4th ed.). London: Nicholas Brealey.

Wiggins, G. (2011). A true test: toward more authentic and equitable assessment. *Phi Delta Kappan, 92*(7), 81–93. https://doi.org/10.1177/003172171109200721

World Health Organization (2010). *Global recommendations on physical activity for health*. WHO Library Cataloguing-in-Publication Data.

Wright, J., & Forrest, G. (2007). A social semiotic analysis of knowledge construction and Games Centred Approaches to teaching. *Physical Education & Sport Pedagogy, 12*(3), 273–287. https://doi.org/10.1080/17408980701610201

2 Practical application of invasion/territory games using the Tactical Games Approach

Invasion games: definition and principles

In invasion games, teams score moving a ball/projectile (e.g., Frisbee, basketball) into the opponents' team field to shoot into a fixed target (e.g., goal, basket) or move the ball/projectile across an open-ended target (e.g., line) (Almond, 1986). Invasion games are highly complex team games that comprise more players per team than other game categories, forcing learners to manage their own location, trajectories of the ball and other players' movements and location with limited time to dribble or pass the ball/projectile into the scoring area and score (Gréhaigne, Caty, & Godbout, 2010), hence producing more complex tactics (Thorpe & Bunker, 1989). Learners can perform two basic roles while playing:

1 **On-the-ball players:** players who control the ball/projectile; they make decisions that respond to the game's demands, trying to solve game situations that determine the continuity or the pattern of the moves (Gréhaigne et al., 2010). These players have four options – run, dribble, pass or shoot (Bayer, 1992) – and the skills used to perform these skills are quite different.
2 **Off-the-ball players:** players who are not in possession of the ball/projectile; they have three options – support, cover or mark – depending on their position in the field.

Invasion games involve individuals playing with other teammates to achieve a common goal, and this partnership can contribute to support diversity in physical literate (Whitehead, 2010). In addition, this teamwork is important for the team to be successful because the decisions and the actions of a single player are dependent on what the rest of the players on the team and the opponents are doing (Tallir, Philippaerts, Valcke, Musch, & Lenoir, 2012).

All these options/actions are performed in different game situations (*offensive tactical principles*):

1 **Maintain ball possession:** when on-the-ball players decide to pass the ball to another teammate, catchable passes do not only depend on the passers' ability but also on off-the-ball players' skills (MacPhail, Kirk, & Griffin, 2008). Support includes tactical moves to have an optimal position on the playing field at the right time (Memmert & Harvey, 2010).
2 **Progress to the goal:** on-the-ball players can progress to the opposite team's goal running, dribbling or passing. This principle includes the tactical requirement of transporting the ball to an area (i.e., goal, end zone) with the help of teammates (Memmert & Harvey, 2010).
3 **Attack the goal:** this action includes the tactical requirements to make temporal and spatial decisions while solving tactical situations (Memmert & Harvey, 2010). Players try to score in different ways, depending on the game/sport they are playing. For example, in basketball, players score making the ball pass through a basket (using the hands), whereas in soccer, players score when they pass the ball through the goal line (using any part of the body except the hands). In hockey, players score similarly to soccer but using an implement to propel the ball into the goal.

At the other end, the defence will try to avoid the offensive team's success. As suggested by Rovegno, Nevett, Brock, and Babiarz (2001), defenders, as a task constraint, add authenticity to the game. When designing games and tasks, different types of defence must be considered, which will progressively hinder the attack. Nevertheless, a strong defence will limit success, and a weak defence will mean no challenge, leading to boredom.

All these options/actions are performed in different game situations (*defensive tactical principles*):

1 **Avoid progression:** defenders will try to avoid the ball/projectile's progression using different types of defence (i.e., man-to-man, zone).
2 **Steal the ball/projectile:** defenders will try to steal the ball, anticipating the opponents' movements, intercepting the pass oneself or by other teammates, or make it go out of bounds.
3 **Avoid the goal:** the goalkeepers (in those sports that have one) have an important role because they are, usually, the last person able to prevent the other team from scoring with specific rules (i.e., use hands) or tools (i.e., different sticks); however, when they are out of place, another player can try to prevent the score.

Invasion games modifications

To adapt the different games/sports to the needs of young learners, instructors are asked to modify the games' requirements and focus on specific learning outcomes. A recent review highlighted that instructors have difficulties planning and designing "appropriate" games (Kinnerk, Harvey, MacDonncha, & Lyons, 2018). The following sections will present some examples on how to modify invasion games to fit young learners' needs.

How can invasion games be modified?

As noted in Chapter 1 (p. 1), games can be modified in three different ways: representation, exaggeration and adaptation (Griffin, Butler, & Sheppard, 2018). This section provides examples of invasion games modified according to these three possibilities:

1 **Representation:** game modifications by representation are 2x2, 3x3, 4x4 . . . any number smaller that the "real" one, in a smaller playing space than the "real" one; the main rules are maintained, but some are streamlined or eliminated or new ones included to facilitate learning (e.g., a "safe area" around a player when they step on the ball).
2 **Exaggeration:** game modifications by exaggeration are 1x2, 2x3, 3x4, 4x2 . . . any combination where there are more offensive than defensive players or vice versa. The number of offensive players is increased (exaggerated) to facilitate ball progression or scoring (success), whereas the number of defenders is increased to work on covering spaces (zoning), defending a player, stopping ball progression and winning back the ball. Other modifications can be made to exaggerate specific outcomes (mentioned in the next section); that is, the goals can be bigger or more goals can be added with the aim of providing more opportunities for successful scoring.
3 **Adaptation:** game modification by adaptation means adjusting the task requirements to fit each learner's needs, providing opportunities for success while also being challenging for everyone (e.g., when a player successfully plays a 3x3 game, while the others do not, the instructor can ask the player to pass the ball with the non-dominant hand). This kind of adaptation is a prerequisite to develop physically literate individuals.

What elements of the game can be modified?

Griffin et al. (2018) suggested that five aspects of the game could be modified to focus on particular tactical problems (see Chapter 1). This section presents examples of these five aspects and aims to show how slight modifications can make a game change:

1. **Rules:** as in any game category, invasion games have specific rules that shape the players' performance. They can be easily modified to obtain specific learning outcomes:
    - Game 1. 3x3 in soccer.
    - Game 2. 3x3 in soccer with similar elements to Game 1 (number of players or playing area) allowing players to take only three steps while dribbling. The restriction (only three steps while dribbling) creates a new game in which players need to perform more passes and off-the-ball movements (i.e., support). At the same time, this game will limit the development of dribbling skills.

2. **Number of players:** it is easy to see the differences between an invasion game such as soccer (10 field players and one goalkeeper) or basketball (five players and no goalkeeper) when considering the number of players. Reducing the number of players can decrease tactical complexity, thus simplifying the decision-making process. A 4x4 game in soccer or 3x3 in basketball can increase participation and help develop skills and tactics. Instructors should consider different combinations to design the game that best suits the purpose of the session. We can design a 2x2 in basketball to focus on passes and off-the-ball movements such as support: it will enhance participation due to the limited number of players (if a player has the ball, the other one should support) but, at the same time, limits the options of each player (only one pass); when a player has the ball, they can only dribble, shoot or pass to a specific player (the one who does not have the ball), limiting tactical decisions. Therefore, instructors must consider the goals and the technical/tactical outcomes to design a game that best fits both. See these examples:
    - Game 1. 3x2 tchoukball game with two goals. This game promotes scoring.
    - Game 2. 2x3 tchoukball game with two goals. This game helps defence over more playing area to regain possession of the ball, making scoring more difficult.

3. **Playing area:** invasion games are played in a variety of environments (e.g., swimming pool for water polo, grass for rugby) with different playing areas sizes (e.g., soccer much bigger than futsal). Altering the

Invasion/territory games and TGA 27

size of the playing area may help players focus on particular aspects of the games:

- Game 1. A 4x4 handball game with no goalkeeper, small goals and a narrow field. The reduced space forces the defence to be closer, thus making scoring more difficult.
- Game 2. A 4x4 handball game with no goalkeeper and small goals played in a bigger area. This gives attackers more space, making defence more difficult.

4   **Equipment:** there exists an enormous variety of invasion games based on the equipment used (i.e., type of ball, type of implement). For beginners, it is important to adapt this equipment to make them feel safe and allow successful performance. Let's take a look at different examples:

- Game 1: 3x3 lacrosse game with institutionalized equipment ("the crosse" or lacrosse stick).
- Game 2: 3x3 lacrosse game with adapted equipment (shorter than the traditional lacrosse stick). The modification in game 2 will allow young players to be successful performing the drills.

5   **Score and/or goal:** both can be modified, easily increasing the number of goals or their size. Two examples:

- Game 1: 4x4 ultimate game with two goals.
- Game 2: 4x4 ultimate game with two goals and two players with one hoop each (acting as moving goals). In this game each team has the option to score in three goals: one fixed and two moving.

Questioning in invasion games

The different ways in which questioning can be conducted (depending on the focus) were explained in Chapter 1. In this section, some examples are presented adapted for invasion games (e.g., see Table 2.1).

Considerations for teaching invasion games

To set a starting point in the teaching/coaching progression of invasion games, Mitchell, Oslin, and Griffin (2003) proposed that instructors must think of the type of invasion game that will be easier for beginner players and will best help them progress. They suggested the following progression:

1   **Possession games:** 2x2 or 3x3 game forms are best for beginners; young players do not have to worry about direction because they move

Table 2.1 Examples of different types of questioning in invasion games.

Type of question	On-the-ball actions/ off-the-ball movements	Examples
Tactical awareness	Support	What can you do to help the on-the-ball player make a pass?
Skill execution	Mark	How can you slow down the attack?
Time	Dribble	When should you dribble?
Space	Mark	Where should the goalkeeper be positioned to stop the ball?
Risk	Dribble, shoot, pass	What options do you have if you receive the ball in this position?
Rationale	Shoot	What should you do when you are this close to the basket? Shoot? Why?

in the space to achieve a goal (e.g., four consecutive passes), and they do not have to worry about going to a specific area to score because there is no goal. We acknowledge Mitchell et al.'s (2003) contribution when exploring some problems that arise during these invasion games. They warn educators that some young learners will experience the following problems:

- They are static when the other team is attacking.
- They assume that they are going to receive the ball only by yelling at their teammates: "Throw it here!"
- They stay close to the player who has the ball, making all players move close to each other, and the game difficult to play.
- They take a lot of time to make decisions.

2 **Games with a goal:** to add complexity, a goal can be added (e.g., a pair of cones) for each team; at the beginning, it should be small with no goalkeeper and, later, bigger with a goalkeeper. The goalkeeper creates a greater challenge for shooting accuracy (at initial stages, consider the use of soft balls to avoid hurting players), and it is recommended to change the player who plays the goalkeeper to let all experience the different roles during games as well as the abilities and decisions required. Mitchell et al. (2003) suggested that educators should be aware of the following:

- Some learners may need several reminders of the goal where they have to score.
- Restrict movement with the ball, or allow no movement at all.

- Insist that the ball/projectile must travel downward and cleanly through the cones.
- Set the type of defence, and teach "restart the game."

3 **Games with a target player:** this player will be placed on the other team's field, and teammates must try to reach them with an early pass to penetrate the defence. The incorporation of this player into a small-sided game helps players work on beating the defence, looking for gaps in the opposing team's defence to perform a pass. Teams score getting the ball/projectile to their target player. In these games, Mitchell et al. (2003) suggested to be aware of the following:

- Learners must understand that the target player is like a goal; that is, they score passing to this player, who is positioned on an end line, and not by throwing at them.
- Target players need to be reminded that they can move to help their partners pass them and not stand still.
- It may be necessary to teach learners how to restart the game (e.g., if a team scores, the target player will return the ball/projectile to the opposite team).

4 **Games with an end zone:** games such as ultimate Frisbee or rugby involve scoring in an end zone and represent increased complexity because players must carry the ball/projectile into the end zone or receive it inside to score. This is why they should be introduced last.

Soccer sessions using the Tactical Games Approach

Soccer is one of the most popular sports around the world and one of the most researched in GCAs (Kinnerk et al., 2018). Learning is complex and takes time (Gréhaigne, Richard, & Griffin, 2005), and for this reason, long interventions are needed to produce positive outcomes. Within the Tactical Games Approach (TGA), several levels of tactical complexity (see Chapter 1 for information about tactical complexity levels) are presented. When learners are able to perform level I, they proceed to experience level II.

The following proposal will comprise six sessions corresponding to level III, and it is based on a team of 12 players in 8x8 soccer. Mitchell, Oslin, and Griffin's (2006) tactical problems in soccer have been considered:

Scoring: players can maintain possession of the ball (e.g., pass the ball, support the ball carrier), attack the goal (e.g., shoot), create space in attack (e.g., use first-time passing) and use space in attack (e.g., dribble).

Prevent scoring: players can defend space (e.g., mark, press), defend the goal (e.g., goalkeeping) and win the ball (e.g., block).

Restart play: players can face throw-in, corner kick and free kick tactical problems.

The TGA (Mitchell et al., 2003) employs the following features:

- Learners play a modified game focused on a particular tactical problem.
- The instructor designs questions to develop tactical and technical awareness.
- Situated practices guide the learner to practice essential skills or movements to solve tactical problems that arise in the initial game or game form.
- A final game is introduced to use the acquired knowledge.

Mitchell et al. (2006) also suggested six levels of tactical complexity in soccer, with different movements and skills for each one. The following sessions are based on level III (see Table 2.2), where Mitchell et al. (2006) proposed the following:

- Score using target players and first-time passing.
- Prevent scoring-avoiding turns and tackling.
- Restart play (e.g., corner).

Table 2.2 Sessions' plan summary.

Session	Tactical problem	Off-the-ball movements	On-the-ball skills
1	Maintain possession of the ball	• Support	• Pass
2	Attack the goal	• Support	• Pass
3	Create space in attack	• Support	• Pass (free) • First-time pass • Dribble
4	Create space in attack	• Support	• First-time pass • Dribble
5	Win the ball	• Pressing defence	• Tackle
6	Restart play	• Support	• First-time pass • Shoot

Session 1

Tactical Problem: maintain possession of the ball.
Session Focus and Objective: provide support to on-the-ball players to facilitate the pass.
GAME 1: 3x3 played in a 25x20 metre (1 metre corresponds to 1.09 yards) playing area with two small goals (no goalkeeper). There are five cone goals 1 metre wide (created with two cones) placed around the playing area.

Goal: teams must try to make three passes through three of the five cone goals before they try to score in the small goal. Players score one point each time they make three passes through the cone goals and an additional point if they score in the small goal.
Sample question:

Where can you move to help on-the-ball players make a pass? To a place where there is no defence.

PRACTICE TASK: 4x2 in a 15x15 metre playing area. The area is divided into four equal squares, and each attacker is placed inside one of the four squares (the player can only move in their square). The two defenders can move in the playing area (the four squares). Attackers will try to perform 10 consecutive passes, and the defenders will try to steal the ball.

GAME 2: 6x6 played in a 50x35 metre playing area with two small goals (no goalkeeper).

Goal: to support on-the-ball players to penetrate the defence using passes.

Session 2

Tactical Problem: attack the goal.
Session Focus and Objective: use a target player to penetrate the defence, moving the ball.
GAME 1: 2x2 with one target player (attacker) and one goalkeeper in one goal in a 20x20 metre playing area.

Goal: attackers will try to pass the ball to the target player (attacker), who will try to shoot to the goal. Offensive team will obtain one point if the target player receives the ball and another one scores the goal.
Sample question:

How can the target player receive the ball? Moving to an open space.

32 *Invasion/territory games and TGA*

PRACTICE TASK: 3x2 and a goalkeeper in one goal in a 15x15 metre playing area. One attacker will be the passer placed in a line (parallel to the goal line). The defence cannot steal the ball from the target player, and they will try to pass to one of the other two attackers. The defence will try to intercept the pass (individual defence), and the off-the-ball attackers will try to move to an open space to receive and shoot to the goal.
GAME 2: repeat game 1.

Session 3

Tactical Problem: create space in attack.
Session Focus and Objective: create space in attack, playing near the sidelines.
GAME 1: 2x2 with two fixed attackers and two small goals, no goalkeeper, in a 20x15 metre playing area. There will be two lines at the sides of the playing area (20 by 1 metre), where fixed attackers will be.

Goal: Teams must try to score with the help of fixed attackers (defence cannot steal the ball from these players). Fixed players can only do first-time passes.
Sample question:

What options do fixed attackers provide? Move the ball faster, and open the field to create space in the offense.

PRACTICE TASK: 3x1 with two fixed attack players, one small goal and no goalkeeper in a 20x15 metre playing area. The fixed attackers will be positioned near the sidelines, and the defence cannot steal the ball from these players. Attackers can only score if the pass comes from the fixed attackers.
GAME 2: 3x3 with two small goals, no goalkeeper, in a 25x20 metre playing area.

Goal: create space in the offense, taking advantage of the fixed attackers.

Session 4

Tactical Problem: create space in offense.
Session Focus and Objective: one-touch passing.
GAME 1: 4x2 in a 20x20 metre playing area.

Goal: Attackers will try to perform five one-touch passes, while the defenders try to steal the ball.

Invasion/territory games and TGA 33

Sample question:

What can you do after passing to a teammate? Move fast to an open space to try to receive the ball again.

PRACTICE TASK: 4x2 in a 10x10 metre playing area (using four cones; see Figure 2.1). Attackers will be placed between two of the cones. Defender will be inside the square. Attackers will try to do five one-touch passes.

GAME 2: 3x3 with two small goals and no goalkeeper.

Goal: progress to the goal with one-touch passing.

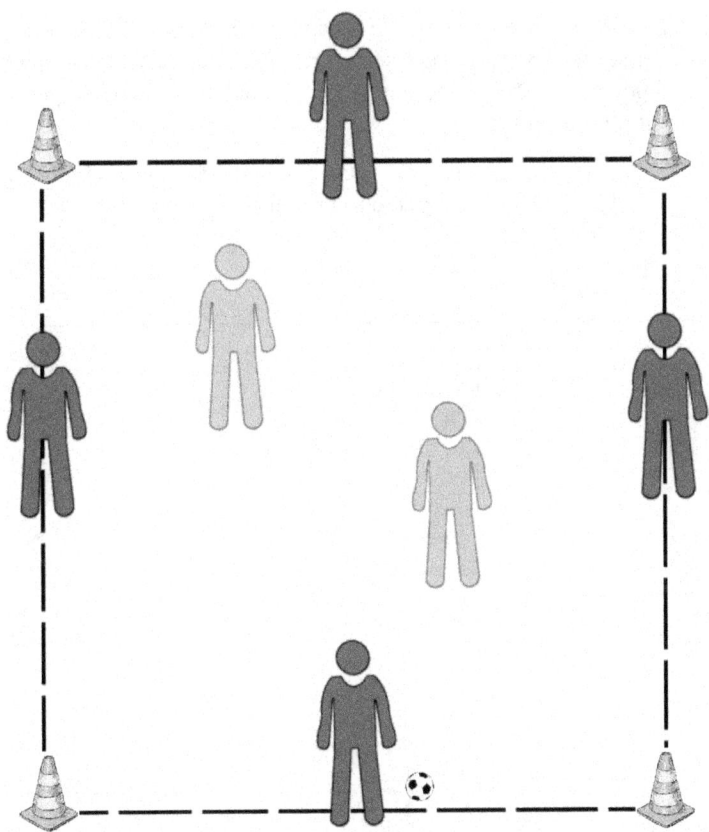

Figure 2.1 Practice task 4v2 in a 10x10 metres playing area.

Session 5

Tactical Problem: win the ball.

Session Focus and Objective: contain offense to avoid progression to the goal.

GAME 1: 3x3 in a 30x15 metre playing area divided in three equal spaces (10x15 metre each) and a small goal without a goalkeeper (see Figure 2.2). Area A is the nearest area to the place where the game starts. Area B is the middle area. Area C is the area where the small goal is placed.

Goal: attackers try to score, and defence tries to steal the ball as near as possible to the beginning line (area A). If they steal the ball in area A, they earn three points; in area B, two points; and in area C, one point. If attackers score in the small goal, defenders do not earn any points. On the other hand, if attackers are able to pass to area B, they gain one point, if they pass to area C, they gain two points, and if they score in the small goal, they win three points.

Sample question:

How can the defence slow down the attackers and win the ball? Pressing and with one-on-one defence.

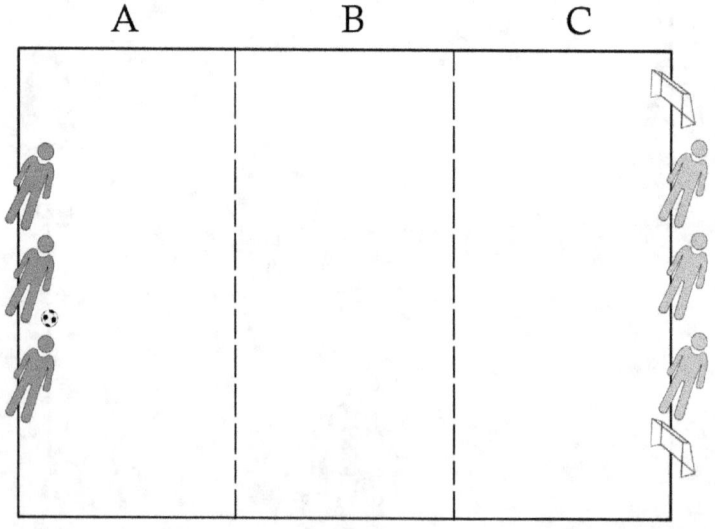

Figure 2.2 Game 1. 3v3 played in a 30x15 metres playing area divided by zones (A, B and C).

PRACTICE TASK: 2x1 in a 10x10 metre playing area. Defender will try to steal the ball in less than 10 seconds.
GAME 2: 6x6 played in a 50x35 metre playing area.

Goal: small sided-game with pressing defence.

Session 6

Tactical Problem: restart play.
Session Focus and Objective: restart the game from the corner.
GAME 1: 4x1 and one goalkeeper (one goal) played in a 15x15 metre playing area. One attacker will be the passer (in one of the corners), and the other three will be placed in front of the goal. The three attackers will be placed: one near the passer, one in the middle and one far from the corner.

Goal: the passer will try to pass to the nearest player, who will try to receive near the left-hand post (if the ball is struck from the left corner) or near the right-hand post (if the ball is struck from the right corner). Once this player has received the ball, they will try to pass to one of the other two players, who will try to score. There will be a maximum of three passes before one player shoots to the goal.
Sample question:

> *How can a corner sent to the left/right-hand post be effective?* The player who receives the ball can pass to the other attackers and create opportunities for shooting.

PRACTICE TASK: 4x0 and one goalkeeper. Similar game to Game 1 but no defenders and two passers. There will be constant passes from the right and left corners.
GAME 2: 3x3 in a 20x20 metre playing area, no goalkeeper and two small goals.

Goal: modified game and reduced playing area. If a goal comes from the corner, it will be a "double goal" (two points).

Teaching adapted invasion games through GCAs

Whitehead (2007) believes that everyone should have the opportunity to become physically literate. That is to say, everyone should have opportunities to be involved in physical activity, regardless of their needs.

There is a lack of research exploring the use of GCAs in adapted sport (Harvey & Jarrett, 2014; Jarrett, Eloi, & Harvey, 2014). Jarrett et al. (2014) designed a series of games for wheelchair rugby. In one of these games, players are required to move around the space in the wheelchair while trying to remove as many tags as possible from their opponents. As suggested earlier in this chapter, games can be adapted to fit the players' needs. For example, a 3x3 game can be used in a wheelchair rugby or basketball session. Similarly, offense can be exaggerated using more offensive players (e.g., 4x2). Game modifications proposed earlier can be used in adapted sports. However, more research is needed in this field of study.

Assessment

Because the concept of GCAs in this book is based on creating physically literate players, not only game performance should be assessed. This section provides some instruments to assess other elements, which can be helpful for instructors.

Motor skill development and tactical knowledge

The change in game concept (from a technique-focused to a game-centred perspective) has led to the development of several instruments to assess game performance in invasion games, not focused on the improvements of isolated skills. In invasion games, the actions performed by off-the-ball players are essential for the team's success (Arias & Castejón, 2012), and hence, assessment instruments should evaluate these actions. In this sense, a physically literate person has the potential to respond appropriately to the demands faced, anticipating movement needs or possibilities and responding appropriately to these with intelligence and imagination (Whitehead, 2010).

The Team Sport Assessment Procedure (TSAP; Gréhaigne, Godbout, & Bouthier, 1997) is popular, but it evaluates behaviours of only the offensive players in possession of the ball. The most widely used is the Game Performance Assessment Instrument (GPAI; Oslin, Mitchell, & Griffin, 1998) because it evaluates offensive players with the ball, off-the-ball movements and decisions.

In soccer, the Game Performance Evaluation Tool (GPET; García-López, González-Víllora, Gutiérrez, & Serra, 2013) assesses technical and tactical skills both on the ball and off the ball in offense and defence. The GPET goes a step further and adopts a situated view to the tactical principles proposed by Bayer (1992) with regard to offense: maintaining possession of the ball, progressing to the opposite team's goal and achieving the objective.

Learners' perceptions can also be evaluated. The Perceived Game-Specific Competence Scale (Forsman et al., 2015) was created to examine players' perceptions of their soccer competence in three dimensions:

- Offensive skills (10 items; e.g., "I can move according to our attacking plays during the game so that my teammates can pass me the ball").
- 1x1 skills (five items; e.g., "In one-on-one situations, I am stronger/faster than my opponent").
- Defensive skills (three items; e.g., "I am able to cover my player in defensive situations during games").

A good perception of one's own strengths (physical competence) can lead to improvements in self-esteem and self-confidence, which in turn contributes to the development of physically literate persons (Whitehead, 2010).

Social dimension

In invasion games, cohesion is important for the team's success. Martin, Carron, Eys, and Loughead (2012) proposed the Cohesion Inventory for Children's Sport Teams to assess cohesion in children's sport teams through items such as "Our team members all share the same goals," "My team gives me the chance to improve my skills" or "I will keep talking to my teammates when the season ends." Professionals should care about the players' well-being, and this instrument can help understand how one player feels inside their team, which would lead them to maintain (or not) the activity throughout their life course: the main outcome of being a physically literate person (Whitehead, 2010).

Summary

This chapter provides practical examples of how to teach/coach invasion games and how tasks and drills can be modified, as well as practical sessions on soccer using TGA. Adapted sports are also mentioned with some possible adaptations. Finally, assessment tools on invasion games are provided.

References

Almond, L. (1986). Reflecting on themes: A games classification. In R. D. Thorpe, D. J. Bunker, & L. Almond (Eds.), *Rethinking games teaching* (pp. 71–77). Loughborough: Department of Physical Education and Sports Sciences of the University of Loughborough.

Arias, J. L., & Castejón, F. J. (2012). Review of the instruments most frequently employed to assess tactics in physical education and youth sports. *Journal of Teaching in Physical Education*, *31*(4), 381–391. https://doi.org/10.1123/jtpe.31.4.381

Bayer, C. (1992). *La enseñanza de los juegos deportivos colectivos*. [Proposed English translation: *The teaching of collective sport games*]. Barcelona, Spain: Hispano Europea.

Forsman, H., Gråstén, A., Blomqvist, M., Davids, K., Liukkonen, J., & Kouttinen, N. (2015). Development and validation of the Perceived Game-Specific Soccer Competence Scale. *Journal of Sports Science*, *34*(14), 1319–1327. https://doi.org/10.1080/02640414.2015.1125518

García-López, L. M., González-Víllora, S., Gutiérrez, D., & Serra, J. (2013). Development and validation of the Game Performance Evaluation Tool (GPET) in soccer. *Revista Iberoamericana de Ciencias del Deporte*, *2*(1), 89–99.

Gréhaigne, J.-F., Caty, D., & Godbout, P. (2010). Modelling ball circulation in invasion team sports: a way to promote learning games through understanding. *Physical Education & Sport Pedagogy*, *15*(3), 257–270. https://doi.org/10.1080/17408980903273139

Gréhaigne, J. F., Godbout, P., & Bouthier, D. (1997). Performance assessment in team sports. *Journal of Teaching in Physical Education*, *16*(4), 500–516. https://doi.org/10.1123/jtpe.16.4.500

Gréhaigne, J. F., Richard, J.-F., & Griffin, L. (2005). *Teaching and learning team sports and games*. New York: Routledge-Falmer.

Griffin, L., Butler, J., & Sheppard, J. (2018). Athlete-centred coaching: Extending the possibilities of a holistic and process-oriented model to athlete development. In S. Pill (Ed.), *Perspectives on athlete-centred coaching* (pp. 9–23). Abingdon, Oxford: Routledge.

Harvey, S., & Jarrett, K. (2014). A review of the Game-Centred Approaches to teaching and coaching literature since 2006. *Physical Education & Sport Pedagogy*, *19*(3), 278–300. https://doi.org/10.1080/17408989.2012.754005

Jarrett, K., Eloi, S., & Harvey, S. (2014). Teaching Games for Understanding (TGfU) as a positive and versatile approach to teaching adapted games. *European Journal of Adapted Physical Activity*, *7*(1), 6–20. https://doi.org/10.5507/euj.2014.001

Kinnerk, P., Harvey, S., MacDonncha, C., & Lyons, M. (2018). A review of the Game-Based Approaches to coaching literature in competitive team sport settings. *Quest*, *70*(4), 401–418. https://doi.org/10.1080/00336297.2018.1439390

MacPhail, A., Kirk, D., & Griffin, L. (2008). Throwing and catching as relational skills in game play: situated learning in a modified game unit. *Journal of Teaching in Physical Education*, *27*(1), 100–115. https://doi.org/10.1123/jtpe.27.1.100

Martin, L., Carron, A., Eys, M., & Loughead, T. (2012). Development of a cohesion inventory for children's sport teams. *Group Dynamics: Theory, Research, and Practice*, *16*(1), 68–79. https://doi.org/10.1037/a0024691

Memmert, D., & Harvey, S. (2010). Identification of non-specific tactical tasks in invasion games. *Physical Education & Sport Pedagogy*, *15*(3), 287–305. https://doi.org/10.1080/17408980903273121

Mitchell, S. A., Oslin, J. L., & Griffin, L. L. (2003). *Sport foundations for elementary physical education: a tactical games approach*. Champaign, IL: Human Kinetics.

Mitchell, S. A., Oslin, J. L., & Griffin, L. L. (2006). *Teaching sport concepts and skills. A Tactical Games Approach*. Champaign, IL: Human Kinetics.

Oslin, J. L., Mitchell, S. A., & Griffin, L. L. (1998). The Game Performance Assessment Instrument (GPAI): Development and preliminary validation. *Journal of Teaching in Physical Education, 17*(2), 231–243. https://doi.org/10.1123/jtpe.17.2.231

Rovegno, I., Nevett, M., Brock, S., & Babiarz, M. (2001). Chapter 7. Teaching and learning basic invasion-game tactics in 4th grade: a descriptive study from situated and constraints theoretical perspectives. *Journal of Teaching in Physical Education, 20*(4), 370–388. https://doi.org/10.1123/jtpe.20.4.370

Tallir, I., Philippaerts, R., Valcke, M., Musch, E., & Lenoir, M. (2012). Learning opportunities in 3 on 3 versus 5 on 5 basketball game play. An application of nonlinear pedagogy. *International Journal of Sport Psychology, 43*(5), 420–437. https://doi.org/10.7352/IJSP2012.43.420

Thorpe, R. D., & Bunker, D. J. (1989). A changing focus in games teaching. In L. Almond (Ed.), *The place of physical education in schools*. London: Kogan.

Whitehead, M. (2007). Physical literacy and its importance to every individual. Conference paper presented at the *National Disability Association of Ireland*, Dublin, January.

Whitehead, M. (2010). *Physical literacy throughout the lifecourse*. Abingdon, Oxford: Routledge.

3 Practical applications of net/wall games using Game Sense

Net/wall games: definition and principles

In net/wall games, teams or players try to score sending an object (i.e., ball, shuttle) into the opponent's playing area and avoid a correct return (Almond, 1986). In offense, players make decisions (i.e., placement, shots) based on their own and the opponents' strengths and weaknesses and on their opponents' positioning. In defence, players will try to prevent scoring by returning the object into the opponent's playing area. These games can be played with or without implements (e.g., racket). Almond (1986) classified these games into (1) net/racket games (e.g., badminton, tennis), (2) net/hand games (e.g., volleyball) and (3) wall games (e.g., squash, rugby fives). These games can be played in singles (e.g., single badminton), doubles (e.g., doubles tennis) or small team games (e.g., volleyball).

While playing, learners can perform two basic roles:

1 **Player/team with ball possession:** tries to score hitting the object into a "clean" area (no opponent(s) close).
2 **Player/team without ball possession:** tries to avoid opponents' score by returning the object correctly.

These two roles involve the technical skills of serve, forehand drive, backhand, volley and smash, which can be performed without an implement (e.g., a racket or shovel) (Fernandez-Rio, 2011).

Contreras-Jordán, García-López, Gutiérrez, del Valle, and Aceña (2007) suggested that there exists common tactical principles in net/wall games:

- Maintain the object in play.
- Take the initiative during the game.
- Score.

Fernandez-Rio (2011) highlighted these tactical principles:

- **Maintain "base area"**: central zone in own playing area (best spot to cover all playing court).
- **Maintain "guard position"**: when using an implement, it should be prepared (ready) to use quickly.
- **Send the object to open areas:** forward, backward, to the side . . . to move the opponent away from their "base area."
- **Hit the object at the right time and using the right technique:** to be precise and effective.
- **Move quickly:** to reach the object and respond.
- **Use your strengths and the opponents' weak points:** load the game to the opponent's backhand or on the weakest opponent (doubles).
- **Coordination:** (in doubles) with the partner to support and cover the weak points.

Net/wall games modifications

For learners to feel successful performers, games should be modified and adapted to fit their needs (Hopper & Bell, 2001).

How can net/wall games be modified?

Three types of modifications can be used to make learning meaningful, as noted in Chapter 1:

1 **Representation:** main rules are maintained, but some can be modified or eliminated to facilitate learning (e.g., during a volleyball game, one bounce could be allowed before returning the ball; a reduced version of volleyball, such as 3x3 could be played).
2 **Exaggeration:** the number of players can be modified to make offense/defence easier (e.g., 2x1 in badminton; 2x3 in volleyball). The playing area can be also exaggerated to focus on specific tactical problems (e.g., long playing area to focus on the "clear" in badminton).
3 **Adaptation:** game requirements are adapted to fit the learners' needs and provide successful experiences (e.g., use an implement). Adaptation is an essential modification for achieving learners' demands and contribute to their enjoyment during practice, a core learning principle for physical literacy through life (Whitehead, 2010).

What elements of the game can be modified?

As suggested in Chapter 1, five elements of the game could be modified to develop players' understanding of a tactical problem (Griffin, Butler, & Sheppard, 2018). To modify net/wall games, the main aim should be reviewed: to hit an object (e.g., shuttle) into a space and avoid a correct return (Griffin, Mitchell, & Oslin, 1997):

1. **Rules:** they can be easily modified to focus on specific elements. For example, allow only one specific hit to be performed (e.g., backhand/forehand) or alternative hits (e.g., in badminton, first – clear, second – drop, third – lob). Players must perform a minimum number of hits (collaboration) before trying to win the point (competition).
2. **Number of players:** net/wall games allow different playing formats: single (e.g., badminton singles), doubles (e.g., tennis doubles) or small-sided team games (e.g., volleyball). These games include fewer numbers of players than invasion games, which means less tactical complexity. However, there exist some exceptions (e.g., 3x3 basketball, an invasion game, involves fewer players than volleyball, a net game). Instructors should design games considering different combinations to match those games to the learners' needs. Altering the number of players causes changes during games. When playing 1x1 in tennis, players must be aware of their own and their opponent's strengths/limitations, whereas playing 2x2 means considering the teammate's strengths and limitations.
3. **Playing area:** playing area modifications are important to teach simple game forms. Mini-courts (i.e., short/wide, long/narrow) might be used, and the one finally utilized will depend on the tactical problems the instructor wants their learners to work on. Playing areas can be marked with cones to allow players to move them (autonomy). Net/wall games can be played in different environments (e.g., sand for volleyball, grass for tennis). Each sport/game presents different playing area sizes (e.g., tennis courts are bigger than badminton's). By altering the size of the playing area, the game demands are changed (Contreras-Jordán et al., 2007):

    - if one's playing area is smaller than the opposite's, defence is easier;
    - long playing areas provide opportunities to work on depth, frontal movements and specific techniques (drops or clears);

- wide playing areas help players work on amplitude, lateral movements and specific techniques (parallel or diagonal shots).

4 **Equipment:** it should be modified attending to the learners' characteristics (e.g., age, level). Following Mitchell, Oslin, and Griffin (2003) and Contreras-Jordán et al. (2007),

- the objects used should be soft and provide an easy bounce. At initial levels, the object should move slowly. The instructor should offer a variety of objects (i.e., smaller, larger) to allow learners to choose based on their own strengths and limitations. This is referred to as "teaching by invitation" (Graham, Holt/Hale, & Parker, 2001);
- when learners use an implement (i.e., racquet), these should be light and have short handles; or
- at initial stages, cones can be used to mark an imaginary net (allowing learners to play with a simple barrier). These cones must be soft to avoid any damage. If nets are used, they should be easily adjustable to avoid losing time and maximize practice. A high net decreases the speed of the game and helps defensive players return the shoot, whereas a low net favours opportunities to score and makes defence more difficult.

5 **Score and/or goal:** marking "scoring areas" helps learners focus on specific spaces in the field away from the defenders. "Prohibited areas," where players cannot score, can also be marked. The scoring system provides learners with information on their competence, thereby helping all learners to become successful. If players can only score points by beating an opponent, low-skilled players may never score. Therefore we recommend the following:

- use collaborative contexts, not only competitive;
- do not use negative scores for mistakes (e.g., −2, −5);
- do not play up to a large number of points (e.g., 10) because it will show big differences among players; or
- use collaborative-competitive games, which include points for collaboration (e.g., five shots before scoring) and for competition (i.e., scoring).

Questioning in net/wall games

As introduced in Chapter 1, there are different ways to create questions to promote learning within GCAs (see Table 3.1).

Table 3.1 Examples of different questions for net/wall games.

Focus	Examples
Tactical awareness	What should you do if you are not able to score?
Skill execution	How can you win a point while playing against other player?
Time	When should you stop and restart a rally?
Space	Where can you throw the ball to make it difficult for your opponent to return it?
Risk	What options do you have if you are near the net?
Rationale	If your opponent is moving you around, where should you move after your own hits? Why?

Considerations for teaching net/wall games

Mitchell et al. (2003) recommended the following progression when teaching net/wall games:

1 **From cooperative to competitive contexts:** in cooperative tasks, learners work with a partner to achieve a common goal. During the early stages, it is important for learners to cooperate to integrate basic skills to play a game. If learners are not able to maintain a rally, it might lead to boredom.
2 **From simple to complex:** for skills, movements, tactical problems and game conditions, initial games should involve only a few skills, rules and as few players as possible. As students gain competence (both using different skills and making decisions), game complexity can be increased. However, initial games (easier) should also provide opportunities to use tactical elements.
3 **From individual (singles) to small group (2x2) and large group (4x4) games:** when there are few players, the tempo slows down, and it is easier to play.

The following progression can be organized using these recommendations (Mitchell et al., 2003):

1 In an initial stage, throw-and-catch games over a net or against the wall should be introduced because they are easy for learners. These games are focused on cooperative situations with simple tasks played within a single-game format. In these games, learners are not worried about their partner trying to win a point but on returning the object over the net. Instructors can engage their learners in discussions focused on ways to be successful in these kinds of games.

2   Incorporate underarm striking and team throw-and-catch games. This means moving from cooperative to competitive games and from simple to complex tactical problems.
3   Incorporate striking with the hand/implement or having more than one contact (e.g., volleyball).

Badminton sessions using Game Sense

Badminton is a racket sport during which players focus their attention on a shuttle and their opponents on anticipating the movements of the shuttle (Casebolt & Zhang, 2020). This sport has been highlighted as a lifelong physical activity popular around the world, although being a competent player is a challenging task (Casebolt & Zhang, 2020). As it is show in Table 3.2., the following proposal comprises six sessions using the session structure proposed by Light (2013) for Game Sense. It combines collaborative and competitive games. Mitchell, Oslin, and Griffin's (2006) tactical problems in badminton have also been used: create space in the opponent's side of net (e.g., overhead clear, service), win the point (e.g., smash), attack as a pair (communication) and defend the space or defend as a pair (e.g., side-defence).

Session 1: basic hits

Activity 1: 1c1 (collaborative) played in a 10x3 metre (1 yard = 0.91 metre) playing area with a 1.5 metre high net. Players try to hit the shuttle as central as possible. They count the number of times they hit the shuttle.

Table 3.2 Badminton sessions' plan summary.

Session	Tactical problem	Main objective	Skills to work on
1	Keep the shuttle in play	Experience different basic shots and when to use them	Basic shots: • Backhand/forehand • Clear/lob • Serve
2			
3	Maintain "guard" position	Base position	Body position
4	Create spaces in offense	The concept of depth	Different shots to move the opponent
5		The concept of laterality	
6	Score	Use different shots and when is the best time to score	Different shots to create scoring opportunities

Aim: learn how and when to perform a clear/lob.
Sample questions:

> *How should you hit if the shuttle comes low?* Bottom-up.
> *What if the shuttle comes high?* Up-bottom.

Modifications:

> *More challenging*: include obstacles to make players pay attention to other elements while moving.
> *Less challenging*: modify net height.

Activity 2: 1c1 (collaborative) played in a 10x3 metre playing area with a 1.5 metre high net. Players try to hit the shuttle to the right/left of their partner using backhand/forehand hits. They count the number of times they hit the shuttle.
Aim: learn how and when to perform a backhand/forehand.
Sample questions:

> *Do you hit with the same side of the racket if the shuttle comes from the right or the left?* No, I turn the racket.
> *When the shuttle is coming far from you, what do you do?* Extend the arm to return the shuttle.

Modifications:

> *More challenging*: alternate backhand/forehand hits.
> *Less challenging*: modify net height.

Activity 3: 1c1 (collaborative) played in a 10x3 metre playing area with a 1.5 metre high net. One "forbidden" zone (4x3 metre from the net) on each court. Players try to return the shuttle as many times as possible without landing the shuttle in the forbidden zone.
Aim: learn when and how to use the clear.
Sample questions:

> *What kind of shot you should perform if the shuttle comes high?* Above the head. *Why?* To send the shuttle to the end of the field and avoid the forbidden zone.
> *If the shuttle comes low?* Bottom-up.

Modifications:

> *More challenging*: less "allowed" playing area.
> *Less challenging*: modify net height.

Activity 4: 2c2 (collaborative) played in a 10x4 metre playing area with a 1.5 metre high net. In pairs, players pass the shuttle and alternate who plays the shot.

Aim: focus on the different elements of the game (e.g., shuttle, net, teammate and other players) and perform different shots.

Sample questions:

> What should you do if it is your turn of hitting the shuttle? I Place on the trajectory on the shuttle and I hit it when it is close to the racket.

Modifications:

> *More challenging*: every partner hits two consecutive times; alternative hits.
> *Less challenging*: modify net height and playing area.

Session 2: basic hits

Activity 1: 1c1 (collaborative) played in a 10x3 metre playing area with a 1.5 metre high net. Player serves five consecutive times, and the other player returns the shuttle.

Aim: practice the serve.

Sample question:

> *What is wrong if you are not able to hit the shuttle?* I move the racket too fast/slow, or I throw the shuttle too near/far.

Modifications:

> *More challenging*: the player tries to serve to different places in the playing area.
> *Less challenging*: modify net height.

Activity 2: 1c1 (collaborative) played in a 10x3 metre playing area with a 1.5 metre high net. One player has the racket and shuttle, and the other is in their playing area with several hoops on the floor (ton the right and left of the player). The one who serves tries to hit the shuttle to the other player's position (each time in one hoop).

Aim: focus on spatial awareness and not only on the shuttle.

Sample question:

> *If you want to avoid the shuttle from dropping to the floor, what do you have to do?* Know the place where my partner stands before hitting the shuttle.

Modifications:

> *More challenging*: aim for an empty hoop, where there is no player.
> *Less challenging*: modify net height.

Activity 3: In a 10x3 metre playing area with a 1.5 metre high net. One player serves 10 consecutive times trying to put the shuttle in a hoop placed on the other side of the net (the other player collects the shuttles and changes roles).

Aim: orientate each foot and the racket head when serving.

Sample question:

> *What foot do you put forward when serving?* It depends on the kind of serve.

Modifications:

> *More challenging*: move the hoop to different spots.
> *Less challenging*: modify net height.

Activity 4: 1x1 in a 10x3 metre playing area with a 1.5 metre high net. If players score while using the serve, they obtain two points.

Aim: score with the serve.

Sample questions: questions from previous activities could be used.

Modifications:

> *More challenging*: serving player closes their eyes when contacting the shuttle to serve.
> *Less challenging*: modify net height.

Session 3: base position

Activity 1: 1c1 (collaborative) in an 8x3 metre playing area with a 1.5 metre high net. In the centre of each playing area (5x3 metre), there is an area parallel to the net (1x3 metre). Players try to return the shuttle with one foot in this area.

Aim: use the centre court (base position) as a starting position when hitting the shuttle.

Sample question:

> *How can you keep the shuttle in play for longer?* Move to the "base area," which is in the centre court.

Modifications:

> *More/less challenging*: modify playing area dimensions.

Activity 2: 1c1 (collaborative) in a 10x3 metre playing area with a 1.5 metre high net. Players try to alternate between clears and drops and return to base position.

Aim: the base position as a defensive/offensive tactical element.

Sample question:

> *How can you return a drop and/or a clear?* Moving to the "base position" (centre of the playing area) to be ready for any shot.

Modifications:

More/less challenging: modify playing area dimensions.

Activity 3: 1x1 in a 10x3 metre playing area with a 1.5 metre high net. A circle is drawn in the centre of each playing area (see Figure 3.1). Before returning the shuttle, the player should put a foot in the circle. If they fail to do so, the other player wins the point.

Activity 4: 1x1 in a 10x3 metre playing area with a 1.5 metre high net. Players try to score as many points as possible.

Aim: to score whilst being aware of own and opponent's positions.

Sample questions: the same as in the previous activities.

Modifications:

More/less challenging: modify playing area dimensions.

Session 4: depth

Activity 1: 1c1 (collaboration) played in a 12x3 metre playing area with a 1.5 metre high net. Each playing area (6x3 metre) is divided in two (3x3 metre), and the farthest zone to the net is "home." Players try to perform the highest number of shots from their "homes."

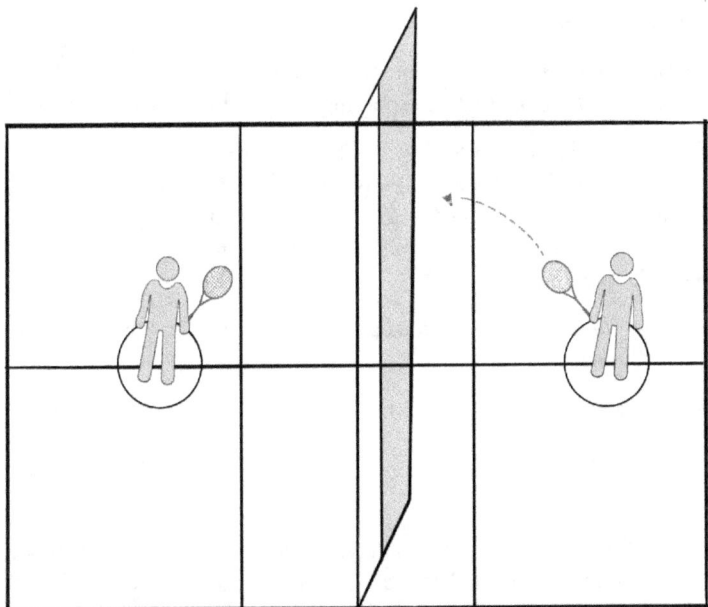

Figure 3.1 Base position game (permission provided by Ramon Friere).

Aim: learn the concept of depth.

Sample questions:

> *What do you have to do to send the shuttle to your partner's "home" area?* Apply the necessary force for the shuttle to get to the end of the field.
>
> *What can you do to keep the rally going?* Place myself where I think the shuttle is going to go.

Modifications:

> *More challenging*: reduce "home"; make the playing field longer.
> *Less challenging*: expand "home"; make the playing field shorter; modify the net's height.

Activity 2: 1x1 played in a 12x3 metre playing area with a 1.5 metre high net. Players try to score, sending the shuttle to a place far from the opponent.

Aim: score by sending the shuttle to an "empty" area.

Sample question:

> *What do you have to do to send the shuttle to the floor far from the opponent?* Anticipate where the opponent is going to be, and send the shuttle far from them.

Modifications:

> *More challenging*: make the playing field longer.
> *Less challenging*: make the playing field shorter, or modify net height.

Activity 3: similar to activity 1, but players try to score as many points as possible. When the shuttle hits the "home" area, the player scores two points; in any other area, scores one point.

Aim: score sending the shuttle to an "empty" area.

Sample question:

> *What do you have to do to score more points?* Send the shuttle to the "home" area.

Modifications: none suggested.

Session 5: laterality

Activity 1: 1c1 (collaborative) played in a 10x4 metre playing area with a 1.5 metre high net. There are four hoops, one in each corner of the playing field (see Figure 3.2). The players try to send the shuttle each time to a different hoop, keeping it in play.

Net/wall games using Game Sense   51

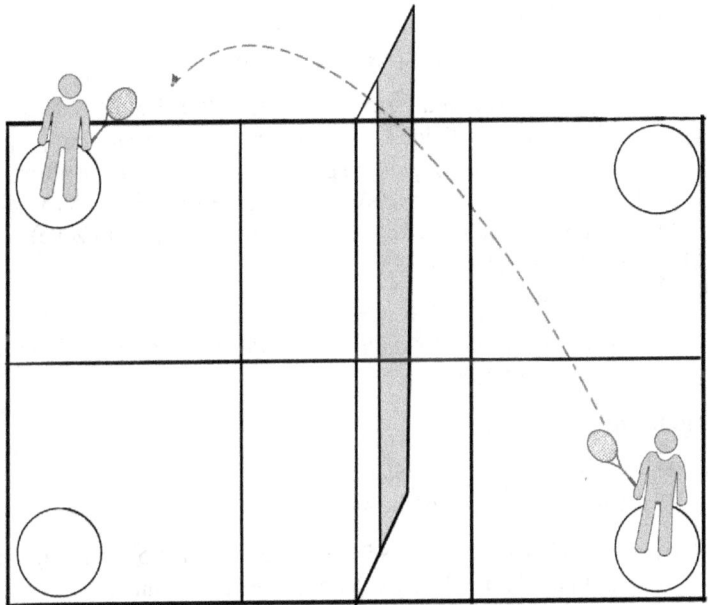

Figure 3.2 Searching for the "Os." Laterality game (permission provided by Ramon Friere).

Aim: lateral throws searching for "empty" areas.
Sample question:
> *What is positive about sending the shuttle to one of the hoops?* You create spaces, and in the next shot, it is easy to find empty areas in the field.

Modifications:
> *More challenging*: send the shuttle to the hoops in order.
> *Less challenging*: modify net's height.

Activity 2: 1x1 played in a 10x4 metre playing area with a 1.5 metre high net. There are four hoops, one in each corner. Players try to score sending the shuttle to the hoop with any kind of shot.
Aim: score sending the shuttle to a limited space.
Sample questions:
> *What do you have to do to send the shuttle to the hoops?* Orient the racket towards the hoop.
> *What kind of hits can you do?* Any.

Modifications:

More challenging: reduce the size of the hoop.
Less challenging: expand the size of the hoop.

Activity 3: 1x1 played in a 10x5 metre area with a 1.5 metre high net. Each player area is divided into five zones (1x5 each one, perpendicular to the net); scoring: more points for the lateral areas; from left to right: two points (first zone), one point (second zone), zero points (third zone), one point (fourth zone) and two points (fifth zone).
Aim: send the shuttle to a selected area.
Sample question:

What can you do for the shuttle to be placed in an area? Point the racket to the selected area.

Modifications:

More challenging: use smaller areas.
Less challenging: modify the net height.

Activity 4: 2x2 played in a 10x5 metre area with a 1.5 metre high net. Shuttles that fall into the lateral areas score two points.
Aim: create space in double games.
Sample question:

How can you score? Moving the opponents.

Modifications:

More challenging: use smaller areas.
Less challenging: modify net height.

Session 6: scoring

Activity 1: 1x1 played in a 10x4 metre playing area with a 1.5 metre high net. Players must think about sending the shuttle near or far from the net, depending on the opponent's position in the field.
Aim: be aware of the best times to score.
Sample question:

When do you decide to finish the game? When I see an empty space in the field (near or far from the net).

Modifications:

More challenging: alternate shots (first near and then far from the net).
Less challenging: modify the size of the playing area.

Activity 2: 1x1 played in a 10x4 metre playing area with a 1.5 metre high net. The first player serves from the centre of their playing area to the centre of the opponent's playing area. They must try to send the shuttle to the server's legs, who tries to return the shuttle. After five tries, players change their roles.

Aim: be aware of the best times to score.

Sample questions:

When it is the best time to send the shuttle fast and down? When the opponent sends the shuttle up.
What do you call this kind of shot? Smash.

Modifications:

More challenging: send the shot to other spots on the field.
Less challenging: modify the playing area or the height of the net.

Activity 3: one player does 10 serves in a 10x4 metre playing area with a 1.5 metre high net. There are six hoops on the other side of the net. The player tries to put the shuttle inside the hoops (one point per hoop). The other player will collect the material and then change roles.

Aim: improve the serve.

Sample questions:

How should you serve to place the shuttle inside the hoops? Strength and precision.
To which hoops can I serve? To those where I think I can score.

Modifications:

More challenging: more points to the hoops which are more difficult to reach.
Less challenging: add more hoops.

Activity 4: 1x1 played in a 10x4 metre playing area with a 1.5 metre high net. There are four hoops, one in each corner. Players try to send the shuttle to a hoop each time. Players must send it five times before scoring. Players earn one point if the shuttle gets to the floor and an extra point if it is in one hoop.

Aim: score by moving the opponent and finding a free position.

Sample questions:

What do you have to do to send the shuttle to the hoop? Point the racket toward the selected area.
When it is the best time to make a smash? When the opponent is in a difficult position to return the shuttle.

Modifications:

More challenging: move the hoop to different places.
Less challenging: modify the playing area or net height.

Activity 5: 2x2 played in a 10x4 metre playing area with a 1.5 metre high net. Players must try to move the opponent to find a free area in the field to score.
Aim: score searching for an empty area.
Sample question:

What do you have to do to find an empty area? Move the opponent.

Modifications:

More/less challenging: modify the playing area or the height of the net.

Teaching adapted net/wall games through GCAs

Despite the lack of research exploring the use of GCAs in adapted sport (Harvey & Jarrett, 2014; Jarrett, Eloi, & Harvey, 2014), currently there are different adapted net/wall sports that can be played with the required adaptations (e.g., standing or sitting volleyball and badminton).

Net/wall games can be adapted in different ways, and here are some suggestions:

- Sitting games can be played with reduced playing areas, first without net and finally with net.
- Learners play a game simulating different disabilities (e.g., only one arm or leg).
- Restrict movement (e.g., sitting, not running) to equate opportunities.
- Give more points to those players with difficulties (when scoring or defending).

Assessment

Because the goal of GCAs is to create physically literate players, we propose different assessment instruments to evaluate learners holistically.

Motor skill development

Rubric for assessing badminton (Casebolt & Zhang, 2020): it contains eight dimensions: (1) badminton smash, (2) badminton high serve, (3) badminton low serve, (4) badminton clear shot, (5) badminton drop shot, (6) shuttle placement, (7) central court position and movement and (8) anticipation skills. Four levels of performance are included in each dimension, with each one having a specific score to rate performance and make the assessment more objective and precise: (1) struggle (one point), (2) developing (two points), (3) meeting (three points) and (4) exceeding (four points).

Cognitive dimension

This aspect involves solving specific scenarios oriented to the understanding of specific situations similar to those faced in games (Mitchell et al., 2003). For example, in 1x1: *Where do you want your next shot to go? What kind of shot would you use?*

We also suggest games invention, which should follow the guidelines suggested by Butler and Hopper (2011, p. 6):

- allow the game to flow;
- provide a structure to which all players can relate;
- provide a safe environment;
- establish fairness;
- involve everyone; and
- make it fun.

The creation of games also contributes to the social dimension, with constant peer debates and discussion.

Social dimension

The use of roles such as captain, conditioning coach or referee, used in other pedagogical models such as sport education (Siedentop, Hastie, & van der Mars, 2020), can be utilized. The use of different roles allows learners to gain autonomy, responsibility and empathy. Recently, Guijarro, MacPhail, González-Víllora, and Arias-Palencia (2020) suggested that roles were an important feature of sport education for developing students' social and personal responsibility at initial stages.

Summary

This chapter provides practical examples of how to teach net/wall games and what kinds of modifications can be performed. Specifically, badminton sessions using the Game Sense framework are presented as well as adaptations for teaching adapted net/wall games. Finally, assessment tools in badminton are also suggested.

References

Almond, L. (1986). Reflecting on themes: a games classification. In R. D. Thorpe, D. J. Bunker, & L. Almond (Eds.), *Rethinking games teaching* (pp. 71–77). Loughborough: Department of Physical Education and Sports Sciences of the University of Loughborough.

Butler, J., & Hopper, T. (2011). Inventing net/wall games for all students. *Active & Healthy, 18*(3), 5–9.

Casebolt, K., & Zhang, P. (2020). An authentic badminton game performance assessment rubric. *Strategies: A Journal for Physical and Sport Educators, 33*(1), 8–13. https://doi.org/10.1080/08924562.2019.1680329

Contreras-Jordán, O. R., García-López, L. M., Gutiérrez, D., del Valle, M. S., & Aceña, R. M. (2007). *Iniciación a los deportes de raqueta. La enseñanza de los deportes de red y muro desde un enfoque constructivista* [Proposed English translation: *Introduction to racket sports. Teaching of net-wall sports from a constructivist approach*]. Badalona, Spain: Paidotribo.

Fernandez-Rio, J. (2011). La enseñanza del Bádminton a través de la hibridación de los modelos de Aprendizaje cooperativo, Táctico y Educación Deportiva y del uso de materiales autoconstruidos [Proposed English translation: *Teaching badminton through the hybridization of cooperative learning, tactical model and sport education and the use of self-constructed material*]. In A. Méndez Giménez (coord.), *Modelos actuales de iniciación deportiva: Unidades didácticas sobre juegos y deportes de cancha dividida* (pp. 193–236). Sevilla: Wanceulen.

Graham, G., Holt/Hale, S., & Parker, M. (2001). *Children moving: a reflective approach to teaching physical education* (5th ed.). Mountain View, CA: Mayfield.

Griffin, L., Butler, J., & Sheppard, J. (2018). Athlete-centred coaching: extending the possibilities of a holistic and process-oriented model to athlete development. In S. Pill (Ed.), *Perspectives on athlete-centred coaching* (pp. 9–23). Abingdon, Oxford: Routledge.

Griffin, L., Mitchell, S., & Oslin, J. (1997). *Teaching sport concepts and skills: a tactical games approach*. Champaign, IL: Human Kinetics.

Guijarro, E., MacPhail, A., González-Víllora, S., & Arias-Palencia, N. M. (2020). Relationship between personal and social responsibility and the roles undertaken in Sport Education. *Journal of Teaching in Physical Education*. https://doi.org/10.1123/jtpe.2019-0097

Harvey, S., & Jarrett, K. (2014). A review of the Game-Centred Approaches to teaching and coaching literature since 2006. *Physical Education & Sport Pedagogy, 19*(3), 278–300. https://doi.org/10.1080/17408989.2012.754005

Hopper, T., & Bell, R. (2001). Games classification system: teaching strategic understanding and tactical awareness. *The California Association for Health, Physical Education, Recreation and Dance, 66*(4), 14–19.

Jarrett, K., Eloi, S., & Harvey, S. (2014). Teaching Games for Understanding (TGfU) as a positive and versatile approach to teaching adapted games. *European Journal of Adapted Physical Activity, 7*(1), 6–20. https://doi.org/10.5507/euj.2014.001

Light, R. (2013). *Game Sense. Pedagogy for performance, participation and enjoyment*. Abingdon, Oxford: Routledge.

Mitchell, S. A., Oslin, J. L., & Griffin, L. L. (2003). *Sport foundations for elementary physical education: a tactical games approach*. Champaign, IL: Human Kinetics.

Mitchell, S. A., Oslin, J. L., & Griffin, L. L. (2006). *Teaching sport concepts and skills. A tactical games approach*. Champaign, IL: Human Kinetics.

Siedentop, D., Hastie, P. A., & van der Mars, H. (2020). *Complete guide to Sport Education* (3rd ed.). Champaign, IL: Human Kinetics.

Whitehead, M. (2010). *Physical literacy throughout the lifecourse*. Abingdon, Oxford: Routledge.

4 Practical application of the Developmental Game Stage Model on striking/fielding games

Striking/fielding games: definition and principles

This game category is referred to as *fielding/run-scoring* (Werner & Almond, 1990) or *batting and fielding games* (Hopper & Bell, 2001). It includes those games with two basic aims: (1) to score points striking an object (normally a ball) and running to specific areas and (2) to prevent scoring by stopping the play, retrieving and returning the struck object (Webb, Pearson, & Forrest, 2006). The most popular games belonging to this category are baseball, softball, kickball and cricket.

Participation in striking/fielding games category is alternative between two teams that share a common space and rotate between the roles of hitters (offensive team) and fielders (defensive team). According to Werner (1989), there are three basic strategies for scoring points (offensive goal) and preventing scoring (defensive goal). Table 4.1 summarizes the main actions of this game category and the basic strategies for both teams.

Striking/fielding games modifications

Adaptations should be made in striking/fielding games to create more game-play opportunities (Mitchell, Oslin, & Griffin, 2003). To reach this goal, instructors (i.e., coaches/teachers) should consider the use of different adapted materials or constraints to reinforce specific tactical-technical solutions.

How can striking/fielding games be modified?

Based on the ideas introduced in Chapter 1, some examples on how to modify games to provide meaningful environments are presented:

1 **Representation:** these types of games are usually slow and involve many players standing, waiting for their turn to participate. To reduce

Table 4.1 General actions and tactical-technical components of striking/fielding games.

General actions (Hopper, 1998)	1 Striking player tries to hit an object (e.g., ball) into the playing area. 2 Striking player tries to score, running between specific safe areas after striking the object. 3 Fielding players try to prevent opponents from scoring, catching the object on the fly (in the air) or retrieving the object to the safe area before the opponent player gets there.
Basic offensive and defensive strategies (Werner, 1989)	
Offensive strategies (hitter–runner)	**Defensive strategies (fielders)**
• Making contact (hitting the object) • Placing the ball in open spaces • Learning when to hit long or short	• Positioning • Preventing running • Fielding (where to throw)

the waiting time effect, fewer players in reduced playing areas are suggested. That is to say, increase the number of games with fewer players than a conventional game.

2   **Exaggeration:** if the instructors' goal is to provide opportunities for attackers to be successful, more players on offense will produce several hitters and, thus, several opportunities to make runs.

3   **Adaptation:** individuals playing the same modified game can develop different skills. For example, in a 4v4, each hitter can choose the ball they are going to hit based on their specific needs and development.

What elements of the game can be modified?

Considering the basic offensive and defensive strategies, as well as the adequate tactical-technical progression in this category, coaches/teachers should try to create effective modified games adapting important game features such as number of players, size of the playing field or rotation of the teams. This section provides some examples of possible adaptations following the five elements proposed by Griffin, Butler, and Sheppard (2018):

1   **Rules:** although softball is played with a specific ball, this ball can be changed based on the learners' needs. Each player/student can choose a ball to hit depending on their expertise. More hits can also be allowed to avoid learners' early elimination.

2   **Number of players:** following Mitchell et al.'s (2003) recommendations, the number of players is the first modification that

instructors should consider. This will be determined by the focus of the session. Sessions where there is a large number of players during the first learning stages will make for poor sessions because learners often have difficulties hitting the ball, which means they have to wait longer for their turn to hit. Increasing the number of games and reducing the number of players will contribute to reduce this waiting time effect.

3 **Playing area:** field sizes can be shorter (attending to the students' age and characteristics) to reduce the distance between bases; the number of bases can also be reduced.
4 **Equipment:** safety is important when designing games. Equipment should fit learners' characteristics. The implement should be light, and it is important to work on how to drop it to the floor after a hit. The instructors should decide if gloves are needed. The balls can be easily adapted by providing learners with the opportunity to hit different balls and choose which one to hit. This will make them feel safer and be more successful. Larger balls are easy to kick but usually travel a shorter distance than small balls, which can travel longer distances but are more difficult to hit.
5 **Score and/or goal:** as previously suggested, the balls can be adapted to fit learners' requirements. Distance between bases can be also modified depending of the main goal of the session.

Questioning in striking/fielding games

This section provides several examples of questions (see Chapter 1) that can be asked in these types of games. First, instructors should be aware of the general actions and basic offensive-defensive principles of this game category (see Table 4.2).

Table 4.2 Examples of different questions for striking/fielding games.

Focus	Examples
Tactical awareness	*What should you do to get to first base?*
Skill execution	*How can you avoid the other team from scoring a run?*
Time	*When should you run to the next base?*
Space	*Where should you send the ball in this situation?*
Risk	*What options do you have if there is no runner at first base and you are going to bat?*
Rationale	*Are you stopping attackers' runs? Why?*

The Developmental Game Stage Model 61

Table 4.3 Common tactical-technical elements based on the level of complexity on striking/fielding games.

Level	Team	Tactical problem	Tactical-technical solution
Low	Offensive	Hit objects accurately into the playing field	Use proper striking mechanics with adequate force
Low	Offensive	Avoid being "kicked out"	Run quickly to a safe area or hit the object to the ground
Medium	Offensive	Score runs	Use different striking techniques to help teammates move closer to the scoring area (steal bases)
Medium	Offensive	Place objects away from fielders	Hit the object into open areas away from fielders
Medium	Defensive	Make hitting the object (ball) difficult	Change the spin, speed and direction of the object (ball)
Medium	Defensive	Cover maximum space	Work together to cover as much space as possible
High	Defensive	Stop run scoring	Throw the ball to a teammate who can prevent a runner from scoring

Considerations for teaching/coaching striking/fielding games

Table 4.3 presents the most important tactical-technical elements for both teams (offensive and defensive) divided into different complexity levels. This gradual complexity highlights the necessity of effectively progressing from basic tactical-technical problems to more complex ones.

At initial stages, all learners should have plenty of opportunities to experience all the roles (positions) in striking/fielding games. Specificity should come at subsequent stages. Under no circumstances should specialization happen before late adolescence (Ginsburg et al., 2014).

Softball sessions using the Developmental Games Stage Model

Softball is quite similar to baseball, and both share, for example, the common goal of getting runners across the home plate. They even share the same governing body: the World Baseball Softball Confederation (WBSC). However, each sport uses different materials (e.g., softball ball is larger), techniques (e.g., softball pitchers throw the ball underhand whereas baseball pitchers overhand), rules (e.g., there are seven innings in softball, nine in baseball) and spaces (i.e., fields have different sizes).

Softball features make it a convenient game to introduce striking/fielding games in schools (upper elementary) or among novice athletes (Mitchell, Oslin, & Griffin, 2006). Considering softball's tactical complexity, Mitchell et al. (2006) divided softball techniques into four levels based on three tactical problems: (1) scoring, (2) prevent scoring and (3) communicating. Therefore, learners with different performance levels can improve their skills and techniques in different versions of modified games.

The main goal of the Developmental Games Stage Model (DGSM) is to develop a progressive tactical learning sequence, paying special attention to the athletes/students' satisfaction (Rink, 1993; Belka, 2004). As can be read in Chapter 1, DGSM is structured into four main stages. Table 4.4 shows the evolution of tactical-technical elements from the development of basic skills (stage 1) to the official version to the game (stage 4).

Instructors should move to the next stage only when the previous stage is effectively consolidated among learners (Rink, 1993). It is recommended the use of strategies such as questioning or *freezing the game* to promote the analysis of the best tactical/technical solution of a specific game situation.

Table 4.4 Progression of tactical-technical learning through four stages in DGSM.

Focus	Stage	Definition
Technical development	Single skills (1)	Participants work alone or with a partner to develop a specific skill.
	Combining skills (2)	Participants work in small (collaborative) groups to integrate isolated skills.
Tactical and technical elements	Offensive and defensive play (3)	Tactics and specific tactical elements are introduced in modified game-play situations. Participants learn how to implement specific skills linked to a tactical problem.
	Regulation play (4)	Advanced tactics, complex rules and specific roles (e.g., first baseman or shortstop) are introduced in real game situations of the sport.
		Because in stage 4 an official version of the sport is implemented (Belka, 2004), Rovengo and Bandhauer (2013) proposed to eliminate this stage in physical education or with novice learners in extracurricular settings.

According to Veroni and Brazier (2006), the two important roles on the offensive team are hitter and base runner(s). On the defensive team, there are seven roles according to the different positions on the field: pitcher, catcher, first baseman, second baseman, shortstop, third baseman and outfielders.

The present proposal will try to assist instructors in designing a comprehensive softball syllabus using DGSM. Four generic sessions are suggested based on the three principles and the four developmental game stages outlined earlier. Each generic session is focused on each of the four stages of the model, starting with the basic skills that students/athletes must learn before playing softball.

To contextualize this proposal, a group of 16 novice learners with no previous experience playing softball were considered. One of them is a player with cerebral palsy and moves using a wheelchair. They can move their head and hands but cannot run or walk, highlighting the premise that everybody has the right to increase their physical, cognitive and sport competence independently of their physical and/or cognitive characteristics (Whitehead, 2010). Some examples of adaptations made for this player are provided in the section "Teaching adapted striking/fielding games through GCAs." All sessions will be carried out on a seven-a-side football pitch, organizing the space in a typical softball diamond distribution and using strike zone mats, cones and/or plastic delimitation lines.

Generic session 1. Stage 1: single skills (running)

Running the bases (offensive) as well as running to catch the ball (defensive) are the first isolated skills that participants need to practice in the first stage. Modified games should be designed to develop a fast and efficient running technique. Regarding base runners, each base should be approached maintaining momentum and minimizing abrupt angles, using a flat arch (Babe Ruth League, 2020).

Participants will be distributed in four groups of four players. Materials needed include two batting tees, two bats, 16 softballs, two large boxes, two sets of plastic delimitation lines and eight cones (or anti-slip medium plastic rings) to indicate each base in a diamond distribution.

The first modified game is called *Balls to the Box* (García-López, 2006). The goal is to score as many runs as possible until the fielding team has put all the balls in a box placed in the middle of the diamond. This game is represented in Figure 4.1. Each player from the running team bats one ball from the batting tee and runs around the bases (without stopping on home plate) until the fielding team retrieves all the balls and puts them in the central box. Roles change: the running team becomes the fielding team and vice versa. The winning team is the one with the most runs.

64 *The Developmental Game Stage Model*

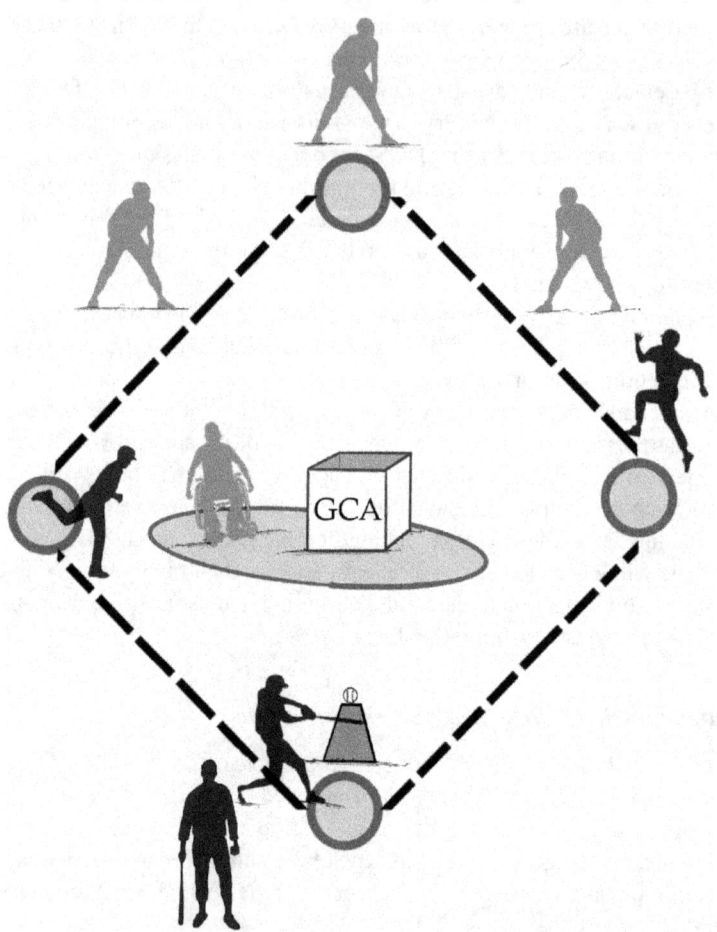

Figure 4.1 Balls to the Box (permission provided by Ramon Freire).

Coaches/teachers can design different modified games to emphasize specific skills and work on different softball drills, bringing in the main characteristics of modified or small-sided games (see Chapter 1). For example, the game *Tunnel and Balls* is based on drills proposed by Graf (2016) and aims to practice running skills. The goal is to score as many runs as possible. The pitcher passes a softball ball to the batter. Then, the batter strikes the ball and runs around the bases (without stopping on home plate) until they hear the word "stop." Meanwhile, the fielding team retrieves the ball, lines up behind the pitcher and passes the ball (with the hand) back to the pitcher. When the pitcher gets the ball, they shouts "stop," and the runner stops running. When all participants have batted the ball, they have to add up all the runs completed.

During game implementation, GCA strategies such as *freezing the game* (i.e., stopping the game but keeping the last position) can help students/athletes see important tactical-technical elements that they have just experienced in the game (e.g., stop the game to analyze abrupt angles during the run).

Generic session 2. Stage 2: combining skills
(basic fielders' techniques)

When isolated skills (e.g., running, throwing, catching, fielding, hitting or tagging) are correctly integrated through modified games at stage 1, the next step is to integrate them. Stage 2 of the DGSM emphasizes the need to integrate isolated skills progressively for students/athletes to see the connections between skills and game play with different tactical problems (Belka, 2004). This progression is essential to create a proper learning sequence from the easiest skills to the combination of advanced skills.

In this generic session, basic fielders' techniques are implemented as an example of how to combine locomotion (i.e., running) with manipulative skills (e.g., catching, throwing or passing the ball) using modified games to combine the skills proposed by Belka (2004). It is important to anticipate ball movement (i.e., direction and power) and to run fast, keeping eye contact with the ball. Materials needed for this session include two bats, two softballs, two sets of plastic delimitation lines and eight cones (to delineate the bases).

One example of a modified game is *Base-ball*. The goal is to pass the batted ball around the four bases before the runner gets to home plate. In groups of eight players distributed into two teams, each player of the fielding team is close to one base, except the pitcher (in front of the home plate). Fielders have to field the ball and throw it to the player next to the first base, who tags the base and throws the ball to the player next to the second base, and so on. If the runner is able to get to home plate before the ball is passed to the pitcher, the offensive team scores one run. If the ball beats the runner, the runner is out.

The aforementioned game can be progressively modified to integrate skills such as communication, considering Belka's (2004) framework. For example, the game can start by asking fielding players to anticipate the direction of the ball and communicate who chases the ball to pass it to first base, while each player gets into position as fast as they can. The combination of basic fielding skills helps individuals learn to catch the ball before it touches the ground (fly ball).

Generic session 3. Stage 3: offensive and defensive play

Sessions in stage 3 are designed to integrate the combination of skills in practical situations using modified games (Mitchell et al., 2013). According to Rink (1993), the implementation of games similar to the official one should be used only when the instructors have checked that the combination of skills have been properly integrated into practice.

The main feature at this stage is that participants play in different situations, for example, a game situation in which the batters automatically have one strike and there is a runner on second base or a game situation in which the team has two outs. These situations are ideal contexts to integrate tactical knowledge with technical skills. It is useful to use laminated situational cards with different tactical problems to solve.

Figure 4.2 shows one example of a game that integrates both offensive and defensive principles: *Tag the Runner*. The goal is to eliminate the runner by tagging them with the ball before they complete a run. Materials needed include one softball, a bat and eight cones or anti-slip rings. Regarding offensive play, this game reinforces the idea of optimizing running, avoiding abrupt changes of direction (stage 1). Regarding defensive play, the game reinforces the importance of covering the maximum space to receive the ball and throw it to a teammate closer to the runner.

Generic session 4. Stage 4: regulation play

Stage 4 should be implemented only when individuals are becoming specialists in the sport (e.g., in specific sports schools such as a softball club) and when the instructor has observed sufficient proficiency to start learning specific roles.

Stage 4 means progressively introducing the most difficult rules of the game, advanced team strategies and specific roles such as pitcher or shortstop. For example, regarding the offensive team, one important role is the *batter* or *hitter*. This role implies specific skills such as hitting behind runners or performing different bunts (e.g., sacrifice, base hit, push, slap, squeeze or bunt and run). On the other hand, regarding the defensive team, the *pitcher* has to manage pop-ups, intentional walks and pitchouts, fly balls, footwork and glove work.

One game that can be played in the first sessions of this stage is the adaptation of *matball* to softball. Materials needed include a bat, a softball ball

The Developmental Game Stage Model 67

Figure 4.2 Tag the Runner (permission provided by Ramon Freire).

and four cones (or four small mats) distributed in a diamond shape. The goal is to score as many runs as possible until the inning ends. When a batter strikes the ball, the runner tries to complete a run before the pitcher receives the ball again. The runners can stop on a base to avoid elimination, but if they are between two bases when the pitcher receives the ball, they are out. When the offensive team accumulates three outs, the inning ends, and the teams change positions. In this game, home runs (completing a run without stopping on any base) score double.

Teaching adapted striking/fielding games through GCAs

Adaptations for a wheelchair player (in practical sessions) can include the following recommendations:

1 Stand near the box to receive the balls from their fielders' teammates and put them in (i.e., in the game *Balls to the Box*), or be the player who throws the ball in other games.
2 Reduce the distance between bases.
3 When the player is moving between bases, the ball should pass twice by every base.
4 Make batting easier (e.g., using a T).
5 Eliminate the player when they are between two bases after touching the ball and counting five seconds. If they manage to reach the base before number five, they continue playing.

Assessment

Tactical and technical dimension

Rink (1993, 2012, 2020) highlighted the importance of carrying out effective observations and assessment during practice to fit the teaching-learning process to the participants' needs. On the one hand, coaches/teachers can adapt a specific assessment tool to assess the most important components of the game (e.g., using the Game Performance Assessment Instrument, GPAI; Mitchell et al., 2013).

On the other hand, they can also create particular (ad hoc) assessment sheets, such as grading game-play rubrics, to record and analyze athletes'/students' progression. According to Brookhart (2018), an ad hoc grading rubric should include four basic components: (1) task description, (2) specific dimensions, (3) a scale including the level of performance and/or the score and (4) a descriptor for each level of performance. Sport ad hoc rubrics must assess the most important tactical-technical components of both teams during play practice. In addition, Mitchell et al. (2013) recommended the design of rubrics which include on-the-ball skills (e.g., pitch, catch, hit or pass) and off-the-ball movements (e.g., run) (see Table 4.5).

Video recording has become a recommended method to help coaches/teachers effectively and accurately assess participants (Lund & Kirk, 2019). It enables coaches/teachers to provide feedback and encourage them during play instead of focusing on the rubric. Additionally, Gabbett, Rubinoff,

Table 4.5 Example of grading game-play rubric for softball.

Name				
Game	4v4 softball game with three innings			
	Needs improvement	*Acceptable performance*	*Good performance*	*Outstanding performance*
	1 point	*2 points*	*3 points*	*4 points*
Throw	• Feet in line. • Body in the wrong position. • Less than 40% of throws on target.	• Steps toward target with opposite foot. • Places throwing arm behind the waist before throwing, does not rotate hips. • 50% of throws on target.	• Steps toward target with the opposite foot. • Places throwing arm behind the waist; rotates hips. • 70% of throws on target.	• Steps toward target with opposite foot. • Places throwing arm behind the waist, rotates hips. • 90% of throws on target.
Catch	• Does not move until the ball hits the floor. • 40% good catches.	• Moves into the path of the ball, sometimes uses correct footwork. • 50% good catches.	• Moves into the path of the ball, correct footwork. • Ready position, watches the ball. • 70% good catches.	• Moves into the path of the ball, correct footwork. • Ready position, watches the ball at all times. • 90% good catches.
Base running	• Overruns bases. • Does not leave the base.	• Precise runs. • Stays on base when the batter hits the ball, no steals.	• Leads off, touching every base. • Wrong decisions to steal.	• Runs the bases correctly (flat arch). • Decides properly when to steal.

Thorburn, and Farrow (2007) showed that when a group of elite fielders analyzed video-recorded plays, they significantly improved their decision-making accuracy and their fast responses in contrast to players who did not participate in the perceptual training based on video analysis.

Social dimension

Sport can also reduce children's violent behaviours and increase their empathy, among other positive values (Koc, 2017), and coaches/teachers should be aware of it during assessment. There are several validated questionnaires or scales that can be used. Bryant (1982) developed the Scale of Empathetic Ability for Children and, consequently, the Index of Empathy for Children and Adolescents.

Summary

DGSM is a GCA that includes the execution of skills first and progressively introduces tactical components. The sessions should be structured following three or four basic stages depending on the participants' skill levels. In addition, a consolidated framework of combining skills has also been proposed to help instructors gradually develop the most important tactical problems and techniques of the specific sports. Finally, summative and formative assessment is highlighted as an important inquiry during the teaching-learning process. Hence, in this chapter, ad hoc grading game-play rubrics and video recording have been analyzed.

References

Babe Ruth League. (2020). *Coaching youth softball*. Champaign, IL: Human Kinetics.

Belka, D. E. (2004). Combining and sequencing games skills. *Journal of Physical Education, Recreation & Dance*, 75(4), 23–27. https://doi.org/10.1080/07303084.2004.10609263

Brookhart, S. M. (2018). Learning is the primary source of coherence in assessment. *Educational Measurement: Issues and Practice*, 37(1), 35–38. https://doi.org/10.1111/emip.12190

Bryant, B. K. (1982). An index of empathy for children and adolescents. *Child Development*, 53(2), 413–425. https://doi.org/10.2307/1128984

Gabbett, T., Rubinoff, M., Thorburn, L., & Farrow, D. (2007). Testing and training anticipation skills in softball fielders. *International Journal of Sport Sciences & Coaching*, 2(1), 15–24. https://doi.org/10.1260/174795407780367159

García-López, L. M. (2006). Las implicaciones cognitivas de la práctica deportiva: constructivismo y enseñanza comprensiva de los deportes [Proposed English translation: *The cognitive implications of sports practice: constructivism and the comprehensive teaching of sports*]. In P. Gil-Madrona & A. López-Corredor (Eds.), *Juego y deporte en el ámbito escolar. Apectos curriculares y actuaciones prácticas* [Proposed translation: "*Games and sports in the educational context. Curricular aspects and practical applications*"] (pp. 207–230). Spain: Ministerio de Educación y Ciencia.

Ginsburg, R. D., Smith, S. R., Danforth, N., Ceranoglu, T. A., Durant, S. A., Kamin, H., . . . Masek, B. (2014). Patterns of specialization in professional

baseball players. *Journal of Clinical Sport Psychology, 8*(3), 261–275. https://doi.org/10.1123/jcsp.2014-0032
Graf, J. (2016). *Practice perfect softball*. Champaign, IL: Human Kinetics.
Griffin, L., Butler, J., & Sheppard, J. (2018). Athlete-centred coaching: extending the possibilities of a holistic and process-oriented model to athlete development. In S. Pill (Ed.), *Perspectives on athlete-centred coaching* (pp. 9–23). Abingdon, Oxford: Routledge.
Hopper. (1998). Teaching games for understanding using progressive principles of play. CAHPER, 27(1), 1–15.
Hopper, T., & Bell, R. (2001). Games classification system: teaching strategic understanding and tactical awareness. *The California Association for Health, Physical Education, Recreation and Dance, 66*(4), 14–19.
Koc, Y. (2017). Relationships between the Physical Education course sportsmanship behaviors with tendency to violence and empathetic ability. *Journal of Education and Learning, 6*(3), 169–180. https://doi.org/10.5539/jel.v6n3p169
Lund, J. L., & Kirk, M. F. (2019). *Performance-based assessment for middle and high school physical education* (3rd ed.). Champaign, IL: Human Kinetics.
Mitchell, S. A., Oslin, J. L., & Griffin, L. L. (2003). *Sport foundations for elementary Physical Education: a tactical games approach*. Champaign, IL: Human Kinetics.
Mitchell, S. A., Oslin, J. L., & Griffin, L. L. (2006). *Teaching sport concepts and skills. A tactical games approach*. Champaign, IL: Human Kinetics.
Mitchell, S. A., Oslin, J. L., & Griffin, L. L. (2013). *Teaching sport concepts and skills: A Tactical Games Approach for ages 7 to 18*. Champaign, IL: Human Kinetics.
Rink, J. E. (1993). *Teaching Physical Education for learning*. New York, United States of America: Mosby.
Rink, J. E. (2012). *Teaching Physical Education for learning* (7th ed.). New York, United States of America: McGraw-Hill Education.
Rink, J. E. (2020). *Teaching Physical Education for learning* (8th ed.). New York, United States of America: McGraw-Hill Education.
Rovegno, I., & Bandhauer, D. (2013). *Elementary physical education: Curriculum and instruction*. Burlington, MA: Jones & Bartlett Learning.
Veroni, K. J., & Brazier, R. (2006). *Coaching fastpitch softball successfully*. Champaign, IL: Human Kinetics.
Webb, P. I., Pearson, P. J., & Forrest, G. (2006). Teaching Games for Understanding (TGfU) in primary and secondary physical education. Conference paper presented at the *ICHPER-SD International Council for Health, Physical Education, Recreation, Sport and Dance*: Wellington, New Zealand.
Werner, E. E. (1989). Teaching games: A tactical perspective. *Journal of Physical Education, Recreation & Dance, 60*(3), 97–101.
Werner, P., & Almond, L. (1990). Models of games education. *Journal of Physical Education, Recreation & Dance, 61*(4), 23–30. https://doi.org/10.1080/07303084.1990.10606501
Whitehead, M. (2010). *Physical literacy throughout the lifecourse*. Abingdon, Oxford: Routledge.

5 Practical applications of Teaching Games for Understanding on target games

Target games: definition and principles

The goal of any target game is to place an object (projectile) in a target area zone to obtain the best score (Webb, Pearson, & Forrest, 2006). To achieve it, specific rules determine the types of actions that are allowed. For example, in some bowling games the ball rolls on the floor, whereas in others it can only touch the floor on the target area a few metres away.

Target games are considered the least complex tactical and technical category (Hastie, 2010). For this reason, Werner, Thorpe, and Bunker (1996) proposed that sports/games should be introduced starting with this category because of its tactical-technical simplicity. Furthermore, Méndez-Giménez, Fernandez-Rio, and Casey (2012) highlighted that an optimal progression is also necessary within target games to promote a comprehensive development of every tactical and technical element. This progression should be in line with the participants' tactical-technical level (influenced by their age or previous experience) as well as their motivation (Peráček & Peráčková, 2018).

Historically target games have been divided in two sub-groups (Ellis, 1983; Mitchell, Oslin, & Griffin, 2003):

1 **Unopposed target games:** these are the simplest tactical and technical games, where participants perform independently sharing the playing space (e.g., golf, archery, bowling or darts), where one player's actions do not affect the opponents' strategy and play.
2 **Opposed target games:** these include more complex tactical elements, and the main feature is that participants can counter-attack opponents' actions either by moving their projectile (e.g., in curling, players can push away the others' rock) or protecting (e.g., in petanque, players can place a boule behind another boule to protect the jack). Other examples are bocce, croquet or billiards.

Méndez-Giménez (2010) and Méndez-Giménez et al. (2012) expanded the target games category to include *moving target games*. The main feature of this sub-category is that the participant's body is the target. Players are normally divided in two teams because the goal is to throw a projectile (traditionally a ball) to the opponents' body while avoiding being hit. Although there is an ongoing debate about the inclusion of this category into physical education and extracurricular sport (Williams, 1992, 1994), it is popular in schools and in children's leisure time around the world through different games: *abki* (India), *British bulldogs* (United Kingdom), *Cheia* (Mozambique), *balón prisionero* or *datchball* (Spain), *matangululu* (Namibia), *filling the bottle* (Zimbabwe), *deweke* (Botswana) or *dodgeball* (United States). According to Belka (2006), abilities such as throwing, dodging, speeding and stopping, catching, fleeing, chasing and moving away or closer to a ball are constantly worked in these games. Moreover, they involve cognitive, perceptual and psychomotor operations because they include the most tactical and technically complex games in the taxonomy (Méndez-Giménez et al., 2012). It integrates offensive and defensive concepts that can be transferred to other categories. Furthermore, it represents the natural step between target and fielding/striking games.

Instructors (i.e., coaches/teachers) should design the syllabus considering the basic tactical principles of this category to create an effective progression. According to Méndez-Giménez (2006), there are four basic tactical principles in *unopposed target games:*

1 **Orientation and positioning:** adopt the correct body orientation and positioning with respect to the target.
2 **Trajectory and power:** choose the right course and power of the projectile (e.g., darts, balls, rocks).
3 **Throw/hit selection:** choose the best throw or hit at the right time.
4 **Projectile placement:** lay the projectile as close to the target as possible or at the right spot.

Opposed target games include the aforementioned four elements but also the following (Méndez-Giménez, 2006):

- **Collaboration:** help a teammate pushing their projectile closer to the target.
- **Protection:** place a projectile to protect another projectile that is closer to the target.
- **Opposition:** throw the projectile to an opponent's projectile to move it away from the target.

Finally, regarding *moving target games,* Belka (2006) identified four tactical principles:

- Be balanced and ready to move.
- Use a variety of fakes.
- Change speed and direction quickly and precisely to avoid being hit.
- Keep visual contact with the projectile.

Méndez-Giménez et al. (2012) suggested the following recommendations for the offensive team:

- Adopt the correct position to shoot.
- Choose the best throw based on the opponents' positions.
- Shoot with accuracy and power.
- Pass the projectile to a teammate who is better positioned.
- Place the team strategically to encircle the opponents.

In relation to the defence team, these are the goals:

- Move away from the opponent/pursuer.
- Find the best route to avoid being hit by the projectile.
- Change direction and speed suddenly and quickly.
- Dodge the projectile, use it as a shield or catch it (depending on the game).

Target games modifications

Despite target games being the "easiest ones," modifications should be made to fit learners' needs.

How can target games be modified?

Different principles can be used, as noted in Chapter 1 (p. 1):

1 **Representation:** the main rules are maintained (e.g., score in a hole in golf), but some are modified to make play easier and provide opportunities for success (e.g., bigger hole). The number of players can be reduced to provide more opportunities to play.
2 **Exaggeration:** some elements can be modified to focus on specific learning outcomes. For example, if the goal of the session is scoring, targets can be bigger to create more opportunities for success.
3 **Adaptation:** if it is too easy or too difficult to be successful, participants can feel bored because the activity is not appealing. The instructor

Teaching Games for Understanding on target games

should adapt the game's requirements to enhance enjoyment, which could contribute to physical activity being practiced throughout the life course (Whitehead, 2010).

What elements of the game can be modified?

Following Griffin, Butler, and Sheppard (2018), five elements of the games can be modified:

1 **Rules:** several rules in target games can be modified to make them more attractive for learners, for example, allowing more options to shoot in archery or darts.
2 **Number of players:** target games can involve low physical activity levels. Instructors should make sure that learners do not wait too long in line. Smaller teams can help.
3 **Playing area:** it is important to consider the playing area to ensure learners' safety. Distance to the target should be adapted to fit learners' needs.
4 **Equipment:** the equipment needed is a target and an object to roll, toss or slide (Mitchell et al., 2003). These can be easily adapted using different ball sizes/material as well as target size (e.g., using a larger target to make it easy to score).
5 **Score and/or goal:** several goals can be used (i.e., boxes, hoops or a target drawn on the floor). It is recommended to adapt the target size to the leaners' skill and experience.

Questioning in target games

There are different ways to create questions to promote learning (see Chapter 1). This section provides some examples for target games (Table 5.1).

Table 5.1 Examples of different questions for target games.

Focus	Examples
Tactical awareness	*What should you do if the hole is far from you?*
Skill execution	*How can you position your body for a better stroke?*
Time	*When should you try to crash your opponent's projectile?*
Space	*Where do you aim to get the ball?*
Risk	*What options do you have if your or your opponent's projectile is in place to win?*
Rationale	*If you aim to score from a farther distance, what kind of stroke is better? Why?*

Considerations for teaching target games

These games are appropriate for young learners because they involve basic skills (Mitchell et al., 2003). Tactical complexity can be adapted to learners' needs, and instructors should adapt their sessions and their games to meet them (Navin, 2016). Sheppard and Mandigo (2003), based on Mitchell et al.'s (2003) progression, proposed the distribution of several tactical problems into three levels of tactical complexity (basic, intermediate and advanced) in target games. Table 5.2 shows the inclusion of the tactical principles previously mentioned within the different tactical problems. These levels of tactical complexity integrate both tactical and technical elements.

Different materials can be used to increase tactical complexity (e.g., ball size/material) and promote safety. Mitchell et al. (2003) recommend the

Table 5.2 Target games' progression of tactical-technical complexity based on Sheppard and Mandigo (2003).

Tactical problems	Tactical principles	Level of tactical complexity		
		Basic (1)	Intermediate (2)	Advanced (3)
Scoring				
Moving closer to target	Orientation and positioning, trajectory and power, throw/hit selection	Aiming for the target with accuracy	Placing the throwing element as close to the area as possible	Pushing own throwing element to the target
Avoiding obstacles	Trajectory and power, throw/hit selection		Using other objects to avoid obstacles	Effects such as spins and turns
Creating a reaction	Collaboration and protection			Contact point
Prevent scoring				
Defending space, moving throwing elements	Protection and opposition		Moving a projectile from the target area	Guarding (protecting an area or a projectile)
Getting the last shot				Giving up one point to get the last throw in the next round

use of barricades to prevent the projectiles crossing to other learners' fields. They also recommended throwing the projectile to the wall and using roles to maximize practice (e.g., resource manager who collects the projectile once it has been thrown). Mitchell et al. (2003) suggested the following progression for target games:

1 **From cooperative to competitive situations:** indirect competition should be considered before including competition against other learners.
2 **From simple to complex:** in skills and tactics.
3 **From unopposed to opposed games:** from simple to complex games.

Target game sessions using Teaching Games for Understanding

The Teaching Games for Understanding (TGfU) model advocates the introduction of the technical elements of the game after experimenting with tactical problems (Graça & Mesquita, 2015). In other words, isolated skill acquisition is implemented only when the participants have discovered the need for it (Webb & Thompson, 1998). Originally, TGfU was structured in six phases (Thorpe & Bunker, 1986):

1 Game.
2 Game appreciation.
3 Tactical awareness.
4 Making appropriate decisions.
5 Skill execution.
6 Performance.

However, Kirk and MacPhail (2002) proposed a redesign of several phrases to reinforce the situational learning strategy. In the hope of facilitating instructors in implementing TGfU, we proposed the reorganization of the sessions. The framework is organized in three phases:

1 *First modified game* form or small-sided and conditioned games (SSCGs).
2 Technical or *skill execution* using drills.
3 *Second modified game* form or SSCGs, reinforcing the skills previously practiced.

78 Teaching Games for Understanding on target games

Each phase is followed by an awareness period to focus on important sport literacy elements using questioning strategies (Harvey, Cope, & Jones, 2016).

- After the first game form (1), *tactical awareness* revolves around the tactical problems being considered. Specifically, instructors guide participants through questions to discover how to solve those problems, and the need to isolate pieces of learning (e.g., a technique) and practice a specific skill. This period introduces the skill execution period (2).
- After the skill execution period (2), *technical awareness* focuses on the technical gestures of the skill performance implemented. As in the first game form, instructors engage participants to internalize the most important gestures to keep in mind when a specific skill is executed.
- Finally, after the second modified game (3), *general awareness* focuses on the most important tactical-technical elements experienced during the session. Instructors invite participants to synthesize the most important elements of the lesson or training.

Figure 5.1 summarizes how a TGfU session should be structured, based on this new version, using adapted boccia (i.e., conventional chairs instead

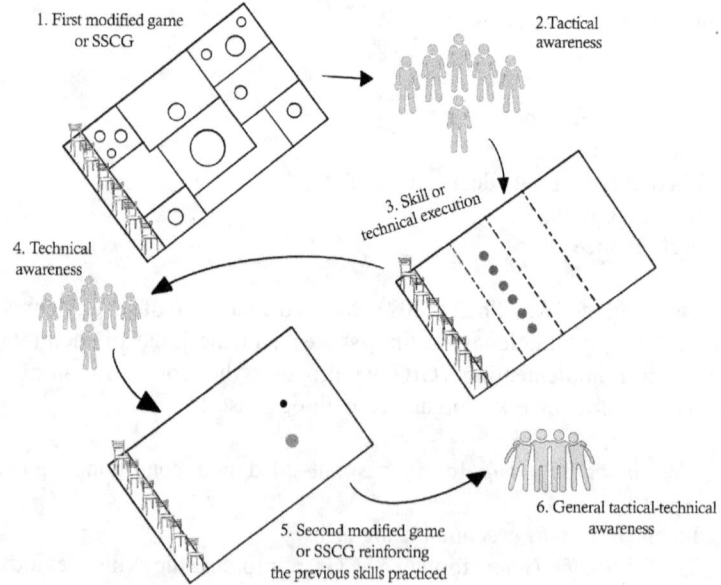

Figure 5.1 TGfU structure in target games.

of wheelchairs) as an example. (1) The *first modified game* aims to place a petanque ball into different areas and into different rings. Then, (a) the *tactical awareness* takes place. The instructor asks tactical questions related to the previous game. Later, (2) the *skill execution* is implemented to reinforce a specific skill or movement patterns, in this case, the petanque throwing technique. Hereunder, (b) *technical awareness* is carried out. Thus, pedagogical inquiry-based strategies are oriented to analyze previous skills and technical issues. Consecutively, (3) the *second modified game* is implemented emphasizing the tactical-technical elements experienced before. In this case, it is an adapted version of boccia. Finally, the session ends up with (c) *global awareness*, reinforcing the most important concepts, tactics and skills experienced in the session. This session is described hereunder.

The aim of the present proposal is to integrate a correct progression of tactical and technical elements through diverse representative targets games based on the taxonomy proposed by Méndez-Giménez et al. (2012) (see "Target games: definition and principles" p. 72). Furthermore, in the hope of understanding how Paralympic sports such as boccia can be implemented through TGfU, this game is used but adapted using conventional chairs and petanque balls.

The session plan is divided into four general sessions. In the first one, the main tactical-technical elements of unopposed target games are introduced using bowling. In the second session, the main elements of opposed target games are introduced with an adaptation of curling. In the third session, boccia (an opposed target game) is introduced to reinforce the idea that everybody can play sports. In the last session, the main tactical-technical elements of moving target games are introduced using shootball (or shootball). Finally, the Game Performance Assessment Instrument (GPAI; Oslin, Mitchell, & Griffin, 1998) is presented as a tool to evaluate tactical and technical elements. These four general sessions can be complemented with other specific sessions following the TGfU structure explained in the first session.

To contextualize this proposal, 18 participants were included. However, one had an arm in a sling following a recent injury. The general adaptation for this athlete, as well as the corresponding teammate, was to throw, kick or roll the ball with the left hand. The same rule was used for the opposing teammates. In moving target games, teams should throw the ball below the waist. Sessions take place on the central futsal pitch of an indoor sports centre. Regarding materials, apart from specific items such as real boccia balls, conventional materials are used. Handmade materials, such as petanque balls with rice and balloons, can also be considered.

80 *Teaching Games for Understanding on target games*

Session 1. Playing bowling: unopposed target game

The main goal is to work on the first tactical level of target games (i.e., orientation and positioning). The second goal is to hit the skittles (or pins) to different sides (central or lateral). The materials needed are: six set of skittles, 18 different weights of bowling balls, three sets of plastic lines to mark the playing area, 24 marker discs (cones) and 12 benches.

During this first session, participants are divided into six groups of three players based on their previous experience and accuracy skills. Each team will be allocated to the most convenient game, where the target distance is different. In the following games and skill drills, two players are in the throwing line, whereas the third is behind the skittles. Their mission is to return the ball to the player along a path marked with the plastic lines and replace the fallen skittles after two consecutive throws. Players rotate.

First modified game form: spare and strike

The aim is to throw two consecutive balls to knock down a set of 10 skittles in a game of 10 frames (20 balls per player). There are six areas of play with lengths from 4 to 8 metres between the throw line and the skittles to meet the participants' skill level. In each game there are different balls (e.g., futsal, basketball, handball or even bowling balls) for participants to experience different sizes and textures. The game finishes when each player has thrown 20 balls. In this collaborative game, there is no competition, and scores are not compared.

For a variation, an area is marked close to the throw line where the ball must land before knocking out the skittles. Fallen skittles are not scored if the ball has not previously touched this area.

Tactical awareness

Participants are gathered in the centre of the field and invited to reflect on the most important tactical elements of the first game. If the questions are not answered correctly, the instructor should clarify the ideas using other words or change the question. Table 5.3 includes questions that instructors can use.

Skill execution: the distance between the skittles

This third part of the session is focused on the throwing technique, which includes important elements such as direction and power. The goal of the

Teaching Games for Understanding on target games   81

Table 5.3 Tactical questions and their possible answers.

Coach-guided tactical questions	Athlete/student answers
Which skittle is easier to knock out?	The one closer to the throw line (skittle number one)
In which direction should you throw the ball to knock down more skittles?	I must point to the centre because it is where there are more skittles
Which direction should you aim at if you want to throw the skittles number 7 and 10?	I must point to the side of number seven to move it laterally and knock down the other one
To make that play, how hard do you have to throw the ball?	I must throw the ball very hard to move the skittle laterally

drill called the *distance between the skittles* is to throw the ball between two skittles without knocking them down. After each throw, the distance between the skittles will be progressively shortened (or vice versa). For this skill drill, benches will be placed to create a path between the skittles and the throw line. In addition, the position of the skittles can be modified, placing the skittles next to one side or in a curved shape. Next, a two-corner skittle skill drill is played: the goal now is to knock down both skittles using one ball.

Technical awareness

In this fourth part of the session, participants are also gathered in the centre of the field and are invited to think carefully about the most important technical actions that they have just practiced. Questions are focused on aiming and throwing techniques. During technical awareness, other pedagogical inquiry-based strategies can be supported with practical examples suggested by participants. Table 5.4 shows a set of questions that can be asked.

Second modified game form: spare and strike with double scores

This second game emphasizes the tactical-technical elements previously practiced. Some variations are added to the initial game: (a) skittles number 1, 2, 3, 5, 8 and 9 score double number of points because aiming for the ball to hit the pocket in between skittles 1 and 3 increases the probability of knocking them all down (strike); (b) triple score is given if there is a corner skittle tactical problem (one skittle on each corner is left) and they are knocked down using only one ball.

Table 5.4 Technical questions and their possible answers of the skill drill practice.

Coach-guided technical questions	Athlete/student answers
Where do you have to aim to not knock down a skittle?	I have to aim for the space between the skittles
Where do you have to stand to throw the ball between the skittles?	In front of the space between them
How do you aim the ball at the space between the skittles?	Looking at the target and placing the ball between the eyes and the target
Where do you move your hand to throw the ball through the skittles?	The hand should make a semicircle before throwing the ball.
Where do you put the leg of the same side of the hand that holds the ball when you throw the ball?	It should be placed back
What can you do to throw the ball hard to hit a skittle to hit another?	Place the ball behind the body and move it forward fast to throw it

Global awareness

In the final part of the session, global awareness is promoted using questions and debates. It focuses on the tactical-technical elements previously practiced: initial positioning and orientation, aiming for the skittles, how to perform a proper bowling throw and how to solve a corner skittle problem (see Table 5.5). Finally, the session can finish with a group greeting.

Session 2. Playing curling: an opposed game

Curling is an opposition game in which two teams of four players slide stones or rocks towards a target area with four concentric circles. There are adapted materials to play curling outside an ice ring (i.e., floorcurling games). In this session, medicine balls have been used (instead of the real curling rocks), and the role of the sweepers with brushes has been eliminated. The aim of this session is to focus on the tactical-technical opposed target game principles (i.e., collaboration, protection and opposition).

The materials needed are 20 medicine balls, three target mats, three large plastic rings, chalk to mark the areas or a set of plastic lines, benches and 24 marker discs (cones). Participants are distributed into six teams of three players.

In each game and skill drill there are two teams of three players at the throw line. When a game is finished, one athlete from each team collects the balls. Each team takes turns rolling their balls.

The first modified game is called *six areas*. The goal is to roll the ball with the hand on the adapted curling area (8 metres), where there are six

Table 5.5 General questions and their possible answers for the final part of the session.

Coach-guided questions	Athlete/student answers
What is the first thing you have to do before throwing the ball?	I have to stand in front of the skittles
Which is the best area to throw the ball if you are throwing with the right hand?	The area between skittles number 1 and 3
And if you are throwing with the left hand?	The area between skittles number 1 and 2
How do you aim the ball for skittles number 1 and 3 or 1 and 2?	Looking at the skittles number 1 and 3 and placing the ball between the eyes and the target
What do you have to look at when you are about to throw the ball?	I must always look at the target—at the skittles that I want to knock out
How can you turn the ball when you throw it?	Turning the wrist when throwing the ball

consecutive zones with different scores. The first one, closest to the throw line, scores one point, the second two points, the third three points, the fourth four points, the fifth three points and the sixth two points. Each team rolls four balls alternatively. Tactical awareness is oriented to think about power and opposition (e.g., "What do I have to do to move an opposing team's ball (or rock)?").

During the skill execution part, power and direction are practiced with a skill drill in which participants try to place the rock into different circles all over the playing space (e.g., central part). Benches can help participants guide the roll. Skill awareness is focused on the technique: slide the rock (e.g., "How do you position yourself to roll the ball?").

The second modified game is called *floorcurling*. The goal, as in the real game, is to roll four medicine balls towards a central target placed in the third quarter of the playing area. To emphasize opposition, if a team manages to move one opponent team's ball outside the target area, two extra points are earned. Finally, global awareness reinforces the most important concepts of this game category (e.g., "If you have one ball left and one opponent's ball is inside the target area, what do you have to do?").

Session 3. Playing boccia: a Paralympic game

Boccia is a Paralympic opposed sport, similar to petanque, played in teams, pairs or individually. The goal is to set the balls closest to a white small target ball called *jack*. The balls can be rolled down a ramp, thrown or kicked depending on the player's special needs. The aim of this session is to put participants in a disabled person's shoes. The second aim is to integrate the tactical-technical principles of unopposed target games with the three principles of opposed target games: collaboration, protection and opposition.

This session is represented in Figure 5.1. The materials needed are three sets of boccia or petanque balls (handball balls and a ping-pong ball for the jack can be used as an alternative), 18 conventional chairs, 20 large and medium plastic rings, three sets of plastic lines or chalk to mark areas and 12 marker discs (cones).

As in the previous session, participants are divided into six teams of three players. In each game, there are two teams. In this case, players should be sitting on a chair behind the throw line to throw the balls with their hands. They can move the chair only before throwing the ball. At the end of each game and skill drill, one player collects the balls.

The first game is called the *five areas*. The game area is divided in five areas (four corners and one central area of 2 square metres). Inside this area, there are medium plastic rings. The goal is to throw six balls to a specific area selected by the instructor. If the balls are inside one plastic ring in the correct area, the score is multiplied by two. Each team takes turns to throw the ball. Questions can be oriented to emphasize the tactical-technical elements of unopposed and opposed games (e.g., "What is more important, hitting an opposing team's ball to get it out of the area or trying to throw your balls into the rings?"). In the skill drill execution, there is a line of red balls in a specific area. The goal is to throw the balls to get them out. An alternative skill drill is to set up different areas and throw the ball to move the red balls to one of them. Technical awareness can include questions related to the throwing technique (e.g., "How do you hold the ball before you throw?").

Finally, the third game form is a representation of the boccia game. The goal is to land the balls as close as possible to the jack. The game is divided into three sets of 12 balls (six per team). In each set, one team starts throwing the jack and takes turns to throw the balls. Global awareness should include questions such as "If it is your last ball and your opposing team has a ball very close to the jack, what should you do?" or "Do you think it is possible to practice sports while sitting in a (wheel)chair?"

Session 4. Shootball: a moving target game

In shootball, the aim is to throw the balls to hit the opposing team's bodies. The field is divided into two identical areas. Each area is subdivided into four sections: one central, two lateral and a base area, which is the farthest from the central line. As observed in Figure 5.2, each team has

Teaching Games for Understanding on target games 85

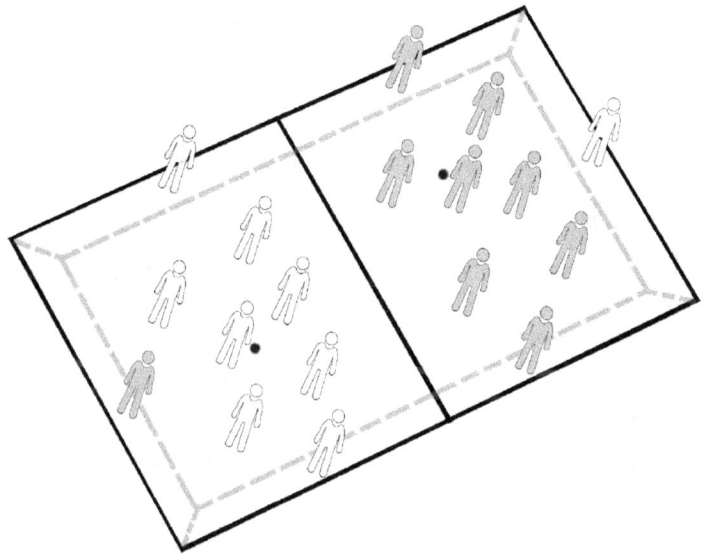

Figure 5.2 The shootball game.

nine central players (placed in the central area), two lateral players (placed in the lateral area) and one base player (placed in the base area behind the opposing team). Two balls are used simultaneously. When the central players are tagged and, consequently, in the base area, lateral players go to the central area to play. If the lateral players are tagged, the base player must go to the central area. The game is finished when the base player is tagged. The role of the lateral players is to recover any ball that is out of the field and pass it to their teammates (they cannot throw the ball to hit the opposing team).

This game can be progressively introduced in several sessions including new roles in each session. For example, in the first modified game, the aim could be to throw to another area as many balls as they can in a limited period of time. The team who ends up with the fewest balls wins the game. Later a target game can be introduced, playing a modified version of shootball using only the central area and introducing the lateral area and lateral players in the following game. Later, the base area and players are introduced.

Regarding technical skills, drills can be designed to learn how to pass while running in a common area or how to throw while changing the distance between moving participants. Finally, skill awareness can focus on the specific skills needed to perform a precise and powerful throw or how to intercept a ball before it falls to the ground (e.g., "How do you throw the ball to avoid it being caught by the opposing team?").

Teaching adapted target games through GCAs

Physical disability

Boccia is probably one of the most popular adapted target game, and it can be played by young learners without significant adaptations (conventional materials can be used to design boccia games).

Intellectual disability

Several recommendations should be considered, including the following:

1 Clear and simple language.
2 Fun environments and an autonomous-support climate.
3 Easy score systems that allows opportunities of success for all.
4 Big, soft and slow projectiles.
5 Big or colourful targets.
6 Demonstrations by the instructors.
7 Use of different parts of the body (e.g., shooting with the feet/hands).

Assessment

Tactical and technical dimension

The Game Performance Assessment Instrument (GPAI; Oslin et al., 1998) is an effective tool to assess participants' behaviours and performance (Memmert & Harvey, 2008). The tool focuses on seven tactical dimensions of game play: (1) decision-making, (2) skill execution, (3) adjusting, (4) covering, (5) supporting, (6) marking or guarding and (7) base position. It can be used in diagnostic, formative and summative assessments.

The instrument consists of two sheets. The first includes the tactical-technical dimensions to be assessed during game play. Each dimension is divided into several items which define appropriate and inappropriate actions. In the second sheet the observer-evaluator records the number of both appropriate and inappropriate actions observed during game play. Finally, the game performance index and the implication of game index can be calculated using simple mathematical formulas.

Teaching Games for Understanding on target games

How to elaborate a specific GPAI for the session plan:

1. The first step is to select the *game dimensions* to be assessed, for instance, decision-making, skill execution and adjusting.
2. The next step is to design an *ideal game* to observe the selected dimensions, such as shootball.
3. The next step is to select which elements of the aforementioned game could be considered appropriate or inappropriate. For instance, for the case of the first dimension, an appropriate decision could be "the player selects and keeps eye contact with the nearest moving target," and an inappropriate decision could be "the player does not select a close target without considering the risk of being tagged." In the case of the second dimension, an appropriate skill execution could be "the player performs a precise and powerful throw considering the distance to the target," and an inappropriate skill execution could be "the player performs a soft throw that can be intercepted." In the third dimension, an appropriate adjustment could be "the player gets as close as possible to the opposite field to throw the ball and moves away without being tagged," and an inappropriate adjust could be "the athlete maintains the same position throughout the game."
4. The next step is to design the *registration sheet* (see Table 5.6). In the present example, the sheet contains two columns for each dimension,

Table 5.6 An example of a GPAI registration sheet.

	GPAI for shootball – registration sheet					
Observer	David			Date		03–03
Player assessed	Peter			Observation		Blue team
Components	Decision-making		Skill execution		Adjustment	
	Appr.	*Inappr.*	*Appr.*	*Inappr.*	*Appr.*	*Inappr.*
Mark with an X o I every moment you observed of the component during the game	XXXXX XXX XXX		XXXXX X	XXXXX XX	XXXXX XXXXX XX	XXX
Total Appr.	8		6		12	
Total Inappr.		3		7		3
Total Observations	13		13		15	

one for appropriate actions and the other for inappropriate ones (e.g., in the case of adjustment, the first column is for appropriate (Appr.) adjustment and the other is for inappropriate (Inappr.) adjustment – see previous step (3).

Finally, the total number of actions is added, and the formulas are used to obtain the game performance index and the individual indexes:

$$\text{Decision making index} = \frac{\text{Appropriate (decision making) actions}}{\text{Appropriate} + \text{Inappropriate actions}} \cdot 100$$

$$\text{Skill execution index} = \frac{\text{Appropriate (skill execution) actions}}{\text{Appropriate} + \text{Inappropriate actions}} \cdot 100$$

$$\text{Adjustment index} = \frac{\text{Appropriate (adjustment) actions}}{\text{Appropriate} + \text{Inappropriate actions}} \cdot 100$$

$$\text{Game performance final index} = \frac{\Sigma \text{ all indexes}}{3}$$

In our example, the sum of all (i.e., Σ) indexes is divided by three because three indexes have been used.

$$\text{Implication of the game index} = \Sigma \text{ every index}$$

Social dimension

Assessment should not focus only on tactical-technical elements. There are positive values that instructors should work on during their sessions. For example, in moving target games it is important to evaluate fair play among participants. Fair play is a set of positive moral values. There are several validated quantitative questionnaires that can be used to assess participants' fair play: the Fair Play Scale in Physical Education and Sport (Hassandra, Goudas, Hatzigeorgiadis, & Theodorakis, 2002) for children and adolescents (6 to 10 years), the Attitudes to Moral Decision-Making in Youth Sport Questionnaire (Lee, Whitehead, & Ntoumanis, 2007) and the Disposition to Cheating in Sports Questionnaire (Ponseti-Verdaguer, Cantallops, Borràs-Rotger, & Garcia-Mas, 2017).

Summary

To sum up, target games are the least complex tactical and technical games. For this reason, using a correct progression, participants can integrate enough resources to transfer knowledge to more complex categories. This would lead to game appreciation and enjoyment, which could lead to the practice of sport/games throughout life, leading to physically literate learners.

References

Belka, D. E. (2006). What do tag games teach? *Teaching Elementary Physical Education*, *17*(3), 35–36.

Ellis, M. (1983). *Similarities and differences in games: a system for classification*. Conference Paper presented at International Association for Physical Education in Higher Education (AIESEP) Conference. Rome, Italy.

Graça, A., & Mesquita, I. (2015). Modelos e conceçôes de ensino dos jogos desportivos [Proposed English translation: *Models and concepts for teaching sports games*]. In F. Tavares (Ed.), *Jogos Desportivos Colectivos Ensinar a Jogar* [Proposed English translation: *Collective sports games. Teach to play*]. Portugal: Editora.

Griffin, L., Butler, J., & Sheppard, J. (2018). Athlete-centred coaching: extending the possibilities of a holistic and process-oriented model to athlete development. In S. Pill (Ed.), *Perspectives on athlete-centred coaching* (pp. 9–23). Abingdon, Oxford: Routledge.

Harvey, S., Cope, E., & Jones, R. (2016). Developing questioning in Game-Centered Approaches. *Journal of Physical Education, Recreation & Dance*, *87*(3), 28–35. https://doi.org/10.1080/07303084.2015.1131212

Hassandra, M., Goudas, M., Hatzigeorgiadis, A., & Theodorakis, Y. (2002). Development of a questionnaire assessing fair play in elementary school physical education. *Athlitiki Psychologia*, *13*, 105–126.

Hastie, P. A. (2010). *Student-designed games: strategies for promoting creativity, cooperation, and skill development*. Champaign, IL: Human Kinetics.

Kirk, D., & MacPhail, A. (2002). Teaching Games for Understanding and situated learning: rethinking the Bunker-Thorpe model. *Journal of teaching in Physical Education*, *21*(2), https://doi.org/177-192. 10.1123/jtpe.21.2.177

Lee, M. J., Whitehead, J., & Ntoumanis, N. (2007). Development of the Attitudes to Moral Decision-making in Youth Sport Questionnaire (AMDYSQ). *Psychology of Sport and Exercise*, *8*(3), 369–392. https://doi.org/10.1016/j.psychsport.2006.12.002

Memmert, D., & Harvey, S. (2008). The Game Performance Assessment Instrument (GPAI): some concerns and solutions for further development. *Journal of Teaching in Physical Education*, *27*(2), 220–240. https://doi.org/10.1123/jtpe.27.2.220

Méndez-Giménez, A. (2006). Los juegos de diana desde un modelo comprensivo – estructural basado en la auto-construcción de materiales: el boomerang en la Educación Física [Proposed English translation: Target games from a comprehensive-structural model based on self-construction of materials: the boomerang in physical education]. *Tándem. Didáctica de la Educación Física*, *20*, 101–111.

Méndez-Giménez, A. (2010). Los juegos deportivos de blanco móvil: propuesta de categorización e implementación desde un enfoque comprensivo, inclusivo y creativo [Proposed English translation: Mobile target sports games: a proposal for categorization and implementation from a comprehensive, inclusive and creative approach]. *Retos: Nuevas Tendencias en Educación Física, Deporte y Recreación, 18*(1), 41–46.

Méndez-Giménez, A., Fernandez-Rio, J., & Casey, A. (2012). Using the TGFU tactical hierarchy to enhance student understanding of game play. Expanding the target games category. *Cultura, Ciencia y Deporte, 7*(20), 135–141. https://doi.org/10.12800/ccd.v7i20.59

Mitchell, S. A., Oslin, J. L., & Griffin, L. L. (2003). *Sport foundations for elementary physical education: a tactical games approach.* Champaign, IL: Human Kinetics.

Navin, A. (2016). *Coaching youth netball: an essential guide for coaches, parents and teachers.* Marlborough: Crowood.

Oslin, J. L., Mitchell, S. A., & Griffin, L. L. (1998). The Game Performance Assessment Instrument (GPAI): development and preliminary validation. *Journal of Teaching in Physical Education, 17*(2), 231–243. https://doi.org/10.1123/jtpe.17.2.231

Peráček, P., & Peráčková, J. (2018). Tactical preparation in sport games and motivational teaching of sport games tactics in physical education lessons and training units. In J. Serra-Olivares (Ed.), *Sport pedagogy: recent approach to technical-tactical alphabetization* (pp. 3–31). London: IntechOpen. https://doi.org/10.5772/intechopen.75204

Ponseti-Verdaguer, F. J., Cantallops, J., Borràs-Rotger, P. A., & Garcia-Mas, A. (2017). Does cheating and gamesmanship to be reconsidered regarding fair-play in grassroots sports? *Revista de Psicología del Deporte, 26*(3), 28–32.

Sheppard, J., & Mandigo, J. L. (2003). *Understanding games by playing games. An illustrative example of Canada's playsport program.* Communication Paper presented at the Second International Conference of Teaching Sport Physical Education and Understanding: Melbourne, Australia.

Thorpe, R. D., & Bunker, D. J. (1986). The curriculum model. In R. Thorpe, D. J. Bunker, & L. Almond (Eds.), *Rethinking games teaching.* Loughborough, United Kingdom: Department of Physical Education and Sports Sciences; University of Loughborough.

Webb, P. I., Pearson, P. J., & Forrest, G. (2006). *Teaching Games for Understanding (TGfU) in primary and secondary physical education.* Conference Paper presented at the ICHPER-SD International Council for Health, Physical Education, Recreation, Sport and Dance. Wellington, New Zealand.

Webb, P. I., & Thompson, C. (1998). *Developing thinking players: game sense in coaching and teaching.* Conference Paper presented at the 1998 National Coaching and Officiating Conference. Melbourne, Commonwealth of Australia.

Werner, P. I, Thorpe, R. D., & Bunker, D. J. (1996). Teaching Games for Understanding: evolution of a model. *Journal of Physical Education, Recreation & Dance, 67*(1), 28–33. https://doi.org/10.1080/07303084.1996.10607176

Whitehead, M. (2010). *Physical literacy throughout the lifecourse*. Abingdon, Oxford: Routledge.
Williams, N. F. (1992). The physical education hall of shame. *Journal of Physical Education, Recreation & Dance, 63*(6), 57–60. https://doi.org/10.1080/07303084.1992.10606620
Williams, N. F. (1994). The physical education hall of shame, part II. *Journal of Physical Education, Recreation & Dance, 65*(2), 17–20. https://doi.org/10.1080/07303084.1994.10606848

6 Practical application of Play Practice on individual games

Individual games: definition and principles

There exist many criteria to classify games/sports. For example, Bouet (1968), from a philosophical perspective, distinguished between athletic sports, ball sports, combat sports, outdoor sports and mechanical sports. However, the most popular classification in sport pedagogy was originally proposed by Ellis (1983) and subsequently revised by Almond (1986). Both classifications are based on common features and tactical-technical elements of games (Silverman, 1997). However, Almond's classification did not consider *individual games/sports* such as athletics, cycling or swimming.

According to Famaey-Lamon, Hebbelinck, and Cadron (1979), the main feature of individual games is that the learners (i.e., players, athletes or participants) are exclusively concentrated on themselves and their own performance. Specific technical elements and physical aspects (e.g., motor learning) are more important than tactical elements (Vigário, Teixeira, & Mendes, 2020).

Besides, participation can be alternative (e.g., javelin throw) or simultaneous (e.g., 100-metre dash) in a common space (e.g., Ironman triathlon) or in separated areas (e.g., swimming). Additionally, variables such as instructor behaviour, positive feedback and instructor control are different in *team games* such as soccer (Baker, Yardley, & Côté, 2003). Finally, it is noteworthy that although these types of games/sports can be taught to a group of learners, their nature presupposes individual performance and personal progression.

Individual games can be classified based on different criteria. Famaey-Lamon et al. (1979) distinguished two main categories based on the learners' cooperative activity:

1 **Individual games without cooperation**, which was also subdivided into four sub-categories:

- **Outdoor sports** (e.g., skiing, swimming, horse riding).
- **Technical sports** (e.g., weightlifting, roller skating, cycling).

- **Ball sports** (e.g., table tennis).
- **Wrestling sports** (e.g., boxing, kung-fu, aikido).

2 **Individual games with cooperation**, which was also subdivided into three sub-categories:

- **Outdoor individual sports** (e.g., alpine climbing, rowing, canoeing, deep sea diving).
- **Technical individual sports** (e.g., team cycling, car rally).
- **Ball sports** (e.g., table tennis doubles game).

According to Famaey-Lamon et al. (1979), the difference between a team in individual games and in collective/team sports (e.g., futsal) is that the ineffective performance of one member of a team in individual sports has a direct negative impact on the result of the team. For example, an error of one participant in a relay race can mean the defeat of the whole team, independently of the individual performance of each participant. In other cases, individual games can be practiced within a team (i.e., racing team), but the victory only has a positive impact on an individual participant. For example, in F1 racing, the aim is to cross the finish line first, regardless of the teammates' positions.

Another way to classify individual games is based on the similarities of techniques, play environment and/or materials (Batalla & Martínez, 2002):

1 **Individual games with similar actions or techniques** (i.e., athletics).
2 **Individual games with similar play environments and materials used for practice** (i.e., gymnastics, surface water sports, outdoor sports, winter sports).
3 **Individual games with similar actions and play environments** (i.e., water sports).

Although a specific game, such as swimming, can be classified in different categories depending on the criteria used, the most important point is to promote a comprehensive progression of the techniques and the tactical elements of the sport through the Game-Centred Approach (GCA) or another meaningful framework.

Individual games modifications

As any other game category, individual games can be modified to fit learners' needs.

How can individual games be modified?

Modifications presented in Chapter 1 focused on other game categories (i.e., invasion/territory, net/wall, striking/fielding or target games), but we believe that those modifications can also be transferred to individual games:

1 **Representation:** learners' success in a safe environment is the essential premise. For example, using the scissors style in high jump or reducing the distance to run in a race.
2 **Exaggeration:** the objective is to focus on specific learning outcomes. For instance, in taekwondo, the attack can be exaggerated by giving different scores depending on the part of the body touched, or defence can be exaggerated giving extra points for blocking two or three consecutive moves.
3 **Adaptation:** it is important to provide opportunities for success during practice. Therefore, different games must be adapted to fit the learners' needs, avoiding impossible or unchallenging goals. For example, this can be achieved setting a height to jump depending on the learners' characteristics and context.

What elements of the game can be modified?

As it was suggested in Chapter 1, five basic elements can be modified:

1 **Rules:** in high jump games, the main objective would be the same as in the elite sport (i.e., jumping as high as you can), but the way to achieve it would be different. For example, the scissors style could be used. In combat games, different hits can be alternated (e.g., arm/leg strokes), and head hits are banned.
2 **Number of players:** cooperative situations can be created, forming teams instead of playing individually. A relay race can help learners feel part of a team during peer tasks in which teammates support partners.
3 **Playing area:** it is easy to see how the playing area can be modified in a long-distance race. Learners must not run elite athletes' distances. The same must happen in the rest of the Olympic disciplines or competitive settings.
4 **Equipment:** learners' safety is a compulsory premise when modifying individual games. The weapon (e.g., sabre) must be adapted not to harm young learners (e.g., using foam noodles). In addition, the weight and height of several objects (e.g., hurdles, javelin) must be adapted for learners to feel safe.

5 **Score and/or goal:** in combat games, different body parts can mean different scores (excepting the head) as well as precision in the stroke. Different challenges can be implemented to increase learners' confidence and satisfaction (e.g., turn the lying opponents' body upwards or downwards). Score systems must provide opportunities for success for all learners based on individual improvements and not on comparative scores (with other partners).

Questioning in individual games

Different questions can promote understanding of the main principles of these types of games (see Chapter 1). Questions in individual games will provide independent problem-solving regarding techniques and tactics (Table 6.1).

Considerations for teaching individual games

As suggested by Launder and Piltz (2013), children do not like to fail, especially if they are in front of their peers. Therefore, when individual games/sports are introduced, the emphasis should be on each learner's performance and not on the comparison. However, traditional approaches compare learners' performances with negative consequences (Launder & Piltz, 2013). In this section, we will try to provide ideas to develop physically literate learners who enjoy the practice and feel confident practicing thes kinds of sports:

- **Learn how to win and lose (respect):** as previously suggested, children do not like to fail or to be beaten (Launder & Piltz, 2013). It is mandatory to create situations in which all learners can achieve some

Table 6.1 Examples of different questions for individual games.

Focus	Examples
Tactical awareness	*What should you do if you want to run the whole distance (long distance)?*
Skill execution	*How can you throw the ball/object as far as you can?*
Time	*When should you start running on a relay race?*
Space	*Where can you throw the javelin if you want to win over your opponents?*
Risk	*What options do you have if you and your teammates are going to run a relay race?*
Rationale	*Why are you adopting this position to run the relay race?*

degree of success. However, some children can get frustrated, and the instructor (i.e., coach/teacher) has an important role to avoid the loss of interest in the game. For this reason, it is important to develop respect and cooperation among young learners.

- **Reducing technical demands in a safety environment:** to help learners succeed it is recommended to adapt complex techniques to learners' characteristics as well as to use materials that increase learners' confidence (e.g., foam floor mats).
- **Challenges:** young learners like to be challenged. This could be achieved through record-keeping, as proposed in sport education (Siedentop, Hastie, & Van der Mars, 2020), with apps such as CoachMyVideo™. The aim of record-keeping should not be to compare with other learners' records but to focus on personal improvements.
- **Every learner has different abilities (process versus product):** young learners must understand that everyone has different abilities (e.g., speed or strength), and these personal characteristics will be used to reinforce individual strengths and work on limitations. Here, the instructor should reinforce the idea of personal effort to achieve personal objectives and progressively overcome personal weakness. Hence, personal improvements must be valued throughout the sessions (process) and not only based on final scores in a specific activity (product). This is called "indirect competition" by Launder and Piltz (2013), understood as children striving to beat their own previous scores rather than others'.

Individual games sessions using Play Practice

Play Practice constitutes a framework to guide instructors to design challenging but safe learning environments across a broad range of games (Launder, 2001). Originally, it was designed for extracurricular environments (coaching) and framed around three main axes: (1) key concepts, (2) principles and (3) operating frameworks. This structure enables instructors to maximize enjoyment and improvement of both tactical and technical elements of the game, in other words, to develop a comprehensive game sense of rules, tactics, strategy and techniques in an adequate environment.

The sessions in play practice must start with a simplified playful challenge or game involving specific techniques considering the progression of the learners as well as providing encouragement. After the game, the instructor and the learners have to reflect and decide which things need to be practice and improved. Then, a specific practice is set up to manipulate key concepts, variables and cues.

During practice, the instructor must provide *positive feedback*, deciding if more practice is needed. The session must culminate in an activity or game to reinforce the most important tactical and technical elements (Launder & Piltz, 2013). However, the play practice structure for individual games has to be adapted to the skills and techniques of those games. Hence, the session must introduce a specific technique as a playful challenge or game. During the game, the instructor has to assess learners' technical development and record the performance and progression. The lessons finish with a final reflection, praising all improvements.

The secrets behind swimming

Aquatic activities like swimming are among the most popular sports in the United States and the UK (Adnan et al., 2020; Dixon & Bixler, 2007; Lazar, Khanna, Chesler, & Salciccioli, 2013). Swimming provides a wide range of valued benefits for health such as physical fitness (Oliveira et al., 2019) and psychological well-being (Szabo et al., 2019). In addition, Mische-Lawson et al. (2019) showed that swimming could be an ideal sport for children with autism spectrum disorders. On the other hand, Lee and Kim (2019) highlighted that swimming enhances life-saving skills in aquatic environments, preventing drowning.

Before mastering a swimming style or stroke, there is a wide range of skills that learners need to learn (American Red Cross, 2014). These skills can be divided into seven categories (Goldsmith, 2015): kicking, breathing, timing and rhythm, turns, head position, body position and catch and arm stroke. Table 6.2 summarizes the main steps to develop each skill effectively as well as the main actions to be corrected during the learning process.

Regarding swimming styles, there are many specific body motion patterns that can be used to propel oneself through water (e.g., sidestroke, doggy paddle or fin swimming). However, there are four main styles based on Olympic and extracurricular swimming competitions: freestyle or front crawl, breaststroke, backstroke and butterfly. Each of these styles integrates five key specific body motion patterns: arms, recovery, body, and head and legs (also called kick). Table 6.3 shows all of them (Mason, 2014).

These moving patterns should be taught *progressively*. Thus, the process of learning a new style should start with the position of the head and body. Then, arms and recovery movement should be introduced in isolation using materials such as pull buoys or swimming noodles. Next, the kick moments should be practiced in isolation using kickboards. Finally, challenges and games should be designed to integrate body movements.

98 Play Practice on individual games

Table 6.2 Guidelines to master the seven basic swimming skills.

Swimming skills	Steps to master the skill	Actions to correct
Kicking	(1) Keep the feet loose; kick the water with relaxed legs. (2) Feel the water "bubbling" in the surface area of the kicks.	Bend the knees too much. Keep the legs stiff.
Breathing	(1) Inhale deeply and normally. (2) Exhale forcefully under the water through the nose and mouth. (3) Leave the corner of the mouth and one ear always in the water when the head is turned to breathe.	Hold the breath or take shallow breaths. Breathe to the front (especially while performing a swimming style).
Head position	(1) Look at the bottom of the pool. (2) Keep the head movement small (especially when the head is turned to breathe).	Lift the head abruptly and too often. Move the head constantly.
Body position	(1) Keep the body, hips and neck in the same line as the head. (2) Maintain evenness and symmetry.	Move up and down. Move from side to side.
Catch and arm stroke	(1) Keep the hands soft and relaxed when they enter the water. (2) Bend the elbow slightly, pulling the arm straight.	Bend the arms too much. Tighten the hands.
Timing and rhythm	(1) Maintain a steady and controlled rhythm.	Focus exclusively on the stroke timing.
Turns	(1) Reach one arm toward the edge wall. (2) Press the chin to the chest to start the turn. (3) Keep the knees together. (4) Perform a forward roll, place both feet on the wall, then push and flip over.	Slow down (decelerate) while approaching the wall. Breathe on the first stroke coming off the wall.

Learning how to teach swimming using Play Practice

This proposal describes a comprehensive and progressive swimming session plan using play practice. To reach this goal, four generic sessions are proposed:

Table 6.3 Specific motion patterns for each swimming style.

Style	Specific motion patterns	
Crawl	Arms	Hands enter the water alternatively above the shoulders. Inside the water, elbows bend and hands move along the side of the body. Hands exit the water slightly above the thigh.
	Recovery	Elbow is bent and high. Hands are close to the water and the body.
	Body	As straight and flat as possible, roll along the axis of the spine with each stroke.
	Head	Keep neutral.
	Legs (kick)	Knees straight and loose, use a constant and rhythmic flutter kick.
Breaststroke	Arms	Scull stroke – hands symmetrically sweep in a sculling motion.
	Recovery	Hands move forward, making a semi-circumference lead by the fingertips.
	Body	Hands and legs do not exit the water.
	Head	Head always points forward, entering the water when arms move forward.
	Legs (kick)	Use a "frog kick."
Backstroke	Arms	Hands alternatively enter the water above shoulders. Inside the water, elbows bend and hands move down along the side of the body to the thigh, led by the thumb.
	Recovery	Elbow moves straight, making a semi-circle outside the water.
	Body	As straight and flat as possible, roll along the axis of the spine with each stroke.
	Head	Head is held upwards, looking straight out.
	Legs (kick)	Use a flutter kick.
Butterfly	Arms	Arms move simultaneously, entering the water with elbows straight. In the water, elbows bend down, pulling the middle of the body outside the water until hands are close to the thigh.
	Recovery	Elbows are straight, making a semi-circle outside the water.
	Body	Make a wave rolling from the head to the feet.
	Head	Push chin to the water's surface to breathe, and head quickly drops to initiate the body roll.
	Legs (kick)	Use the "dolphin kick."

1 **Adjustment to water:** generic session 1: "touching water in the pool."
2 **Postural re-education:** generic session 2: "kicking the legs in the water."
3 **Breathing techniques:** generic session 3: "breathing in the water."
4 **Progressions to introduce a swimming style:** generic session 4: "learning a new style, the crawl or freestyle technique."

Readers are invited to complement these generic sessions with different playful challenges intended to practice or reinforce isolated skills (e.g., backstroke kick) or tactical elements (e.g., how to place swimmers in a relay race).

To contextualize this proposal, a group of 12 learners was suggested. They had not previously attended any swimming classes. In addition, one of them had aquaphobia following a bad experience some years previously at the beach. Sessions took place in a 25-metre-long and 3.5-metre-deep swimming pool. The facility also includes a shallow pool (0.30–1.50-metres deep for children). Participants wore a swimsuit, cap and goggles.

Generic session 1: touching water in the pool

If learning is affected by fear, especially among younger individuals, adaptation is extremely important to help them enjoy the activities in the water (International Swimming Federation, FINA, 2016). The goal of this session is to get learners used to the water, especially for the aquaphobic participant, using playful challenges or games to move learners' attention away from their fears. This session is conducted in the shallow pool. Although this proposal shows only one session, instructors should bear in mind that this process may take several sessions or weeks in the shallow pool, depending on the learners' needs. Materials to be used include floating mats, balls, kickboards, floating noodles and diving rings.

The first challenge is just walking in the swimming pool in all directions, getting around obstacles such as floating balls, pull buoys and foam noodles. Rhythmic songs can indicate the speed of walking. It is important to remind learners that they cannot touch any of the materials because these might move. The instructors will be in the pool to calm anxious learners. Different games can be used in this part of the session: touch and go or moving a ball from one edge to the other.

When all learners have experienced the water below their waist, it is time to introduce the idea of lying on the water. This can cause tension among learners. For this reason, it is important to progressively get their brains used to the new position. There are two basic positions: dorsal flotation (flotation on the back) and ventral flotation (flotation on the front).

Dorsal flotation: the group is divided into pairs. One partner floats on their back, and the other moves them from one edge to the other of the (shallow) swimming pool. They place their hands on the peer's back and head and moves backward. For the aquaphobic case, the exercise is adapted placing a floating mat under them, progressively changing its thickness until they have the confidence to do the challenge without it. The instructor must assess the learner's progression.

Play Practice on individual games 101

Figure 6.1 shows a modification of this challenge in the deep swimming pool. In this case, learners have to pull other learners from one edge to the other in dorsal position (with their face above the water). This challenge can be used only once they are used to shallow pools as well as when basic rescue techniques had been previously introduced. If learners are not used to aquatic environments, the leap from the shallow to the deep pool must

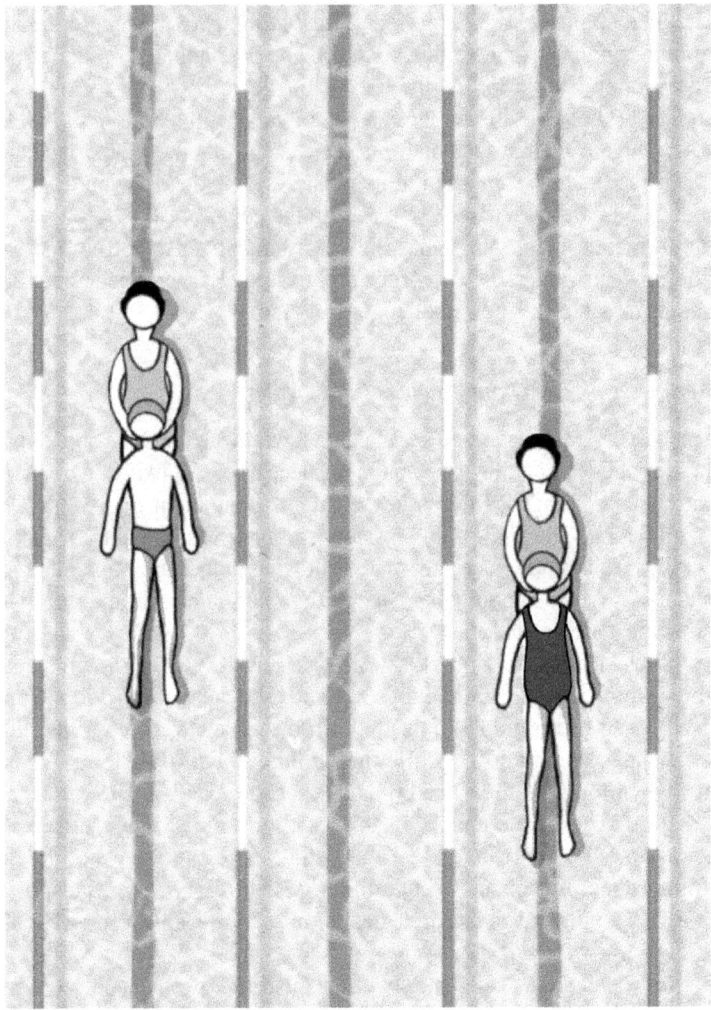

Figure 6.1 A modified game of the familiarization of dorsal flotation in a deep swimming pool (permission provided by Ramon Friere).

not be done until all learners have sufficient confidence and find it a safe environment.

Ventral flotation can be introduced with the following challenge. There are different coloured rings scattered all over the bottom of the shallow pool. Learners have to move horizontally with the head outside the water, "walking with their hands" around the pool. When the instructor calls out a colour, learners have to (horizontally) move and put their hands inside the same coloured ring.

The final challenge of this period of adaptation is to move into the deep swimming pool. To achieve this goal, a game is conducted on the edge of the deep pool. The group is divided in four teams of three learners. The instructor will place different laminated drawings at the bottom of the pool near the edge. One participant from each team puts their head inside the water to see the drawing. Then, they must describe the drawing to the rest of their teammates, who are sitting next to the edge.

Play Practice emphasizes that the environment must be fun and safe. In addition, instructors have to constantly assess learners' behaviours and emotions to determine new challenges or games.

Generic session 2: kicking the legs in the water

When learners are prepared to get in contact with water and are able to jump from the edge in a standing position in the deep pool (FINA, 2016), it is time to introduce kicking skills as a key element to maintain both ventral and dorsal flotation. The goal of this session is to progressively introduce kicking skills through playful games. The following games are implemented in two consecutive deep pool lanes. In addition, 20 foam balls and three large floating mats are needed.

To reach the session's goal, the first game introduces the concept of keeping the feet loose and the legs relaxed. Learners are inside the pool. They have to transport 20 foam balls from one edge to the other, kicking their legs up and down while they hold one ball with their hands in ventral position with their head outside the water. This game can be also played in two or three teams. In this case, the objective is to see who the first is to transport the balls to the other edge. Another modification is to introduce the concept of breathing. When learners are transporting the balls, they have to take their heads out of the water to breathe after 10 kicks.

In the second game, called *the boat*, the goal is to propel a person who is lying on a floating mat from one edge to the other of the swimming pool. The group is divided into three teams of four participants. One of them is the *captain*, the person who is on the mat and decides where to go and when to stop. The rest of the participants have to propel the mat by kicking up and down the water (flutter kick), producing a *boiling* or *bubble effect* in the water. They are at the back of the mat like a motorboat. It is important that this game is played in silence because participants have to hear the orders of the captain, avoiding too much noise with their kicks. Precise kicks do not make too much noise. A modification of this game is to organize a race among the three teams.

Generic session 3: breathing in the water

Launder and Piltz (2013) claimed that breath control in aquatic environments is a fundamental issue, especially for beginners. The specific breathing technique used involves breathing out without lifting the head out of the water while keeping some air in the lungs. Table 6.2 shows the three main guidelines to help participants learn this technique. In addition, breathing skills should be developed alongside head position (see Table 6.2 as well). Although this technique can be learnt using analytical exercises and explanations, play practice assumes the implementation of playful forms to motivate children to learn.

This session is conducted in the deep pool. Learners are divided into three groups of four participants. Each team is placed in three consecutive pool lanes. Twelve kickboards and 12 small foam balls are needed.

First, ventral flotation is introduced in the deep pool by asking learners to transfer a ball placed on a kickboard with the arms outstretched while kicking the legs during two laps (50 metres) and keeping the head out of the water. The second part of the game includes repeating the laps but encouraging learners to periodically put their heads under the water. This game can be finally implemented as a race among the three teams.

The second game is designed to help students learn to turn the head to the side to breathe. Each learner has to transfer one ball from one edge to the other with the arms outstretched (maintaining ventral flotation), kicking the legs, with the head down, turning it to the right side to breathe. The team who first manages to place their three balls on the other edge wins the race. A modification is to change the side to breathe. It is important that instructors assess if learners do not lift their heads too often or if they tend to look too far ahead.

Another interesting game is the duck diving game. The instructor throws in the middle of the pool sticks and rings. One participant of each team has to move with a kickboard using the kicking technique and lateral breath to pick up one and return it to the instructor with the same technique.

Generic session 4: learning a new style, the crawl or freestyle technique

The next step in the learning process is to introduce a swimming style or stroke. However, instructors must be sure that the basic swimming skills have been integrated by their learners. This is why instructors must constantly observe and assess learners' progression using formative or continuous assessment.

This session can be divided in three parts: (1) isolated challenges or playful activities for the body, arms and recovery; (2) isolated challenges for the kick; and (3) playful activities to integrate both patterns. Progressive challenges are introduced to develop the freestyle or front crawl technique. Readers should note that although the progression of the technique is summarized in this generic session, FINA (2016) recommended spending from 12 to 15 sessions of 45 minutes to introduce each style. The materials needed are 12 pull buoys, 12 kickboards and 12 foam balls.

The first challenge is to practice crawl's arm and recovery motion patterns and lateral breathing. First, the instructor explains the technique using visual information (e.g., photo series, slow-motion video), avoiding complex details. Then, the challenge is explained using a question: "Can you transport the pull buoys 50 metres (two laps) between your legs using the crawl arm and recovery technique?" While learners practice the challenge, the instructor assesses whether the basic motion pattern is properly implemented, evaluating whether learners need more practice with other challenges (e.g., correct the recovery pattern using a kickboard and alternatively change the hand which holds the kickboard).

The second challenge aims to practice the flutter kick technique. The instructor explains that an efficient kick does not separate feet more than 30 centimetres. Thus, the challenge is to push a foam ball with the kickboard 50 metres (two laps) using only the flutter kick. In addition, learners are required to breathe laterally after five consecutive kicks. Figure 6.2 shows that the main goal is to transport a ball without touching it with the hands; it must be pushed with the kickboard. Hence, the focus is placed on precise and slow flutter kicks rather than completing the laps quickly and touching the ball with the hands.

Finally, to integrate the techniques, a relay race among three teams of four players can be implemented. If any learner still feels unsafe swimming without any floating material, a floating noodle can be placed around the belly. Considering the specific motion patterns of Table 6.3, similar sessions can be designed for the rest of the styles. Depending on the learners' ages and levels, the distance for each exercise could be increased. In addition, playful challenges can be implemented using foam balls or any other kind of material.

Play Practice on individual games 105

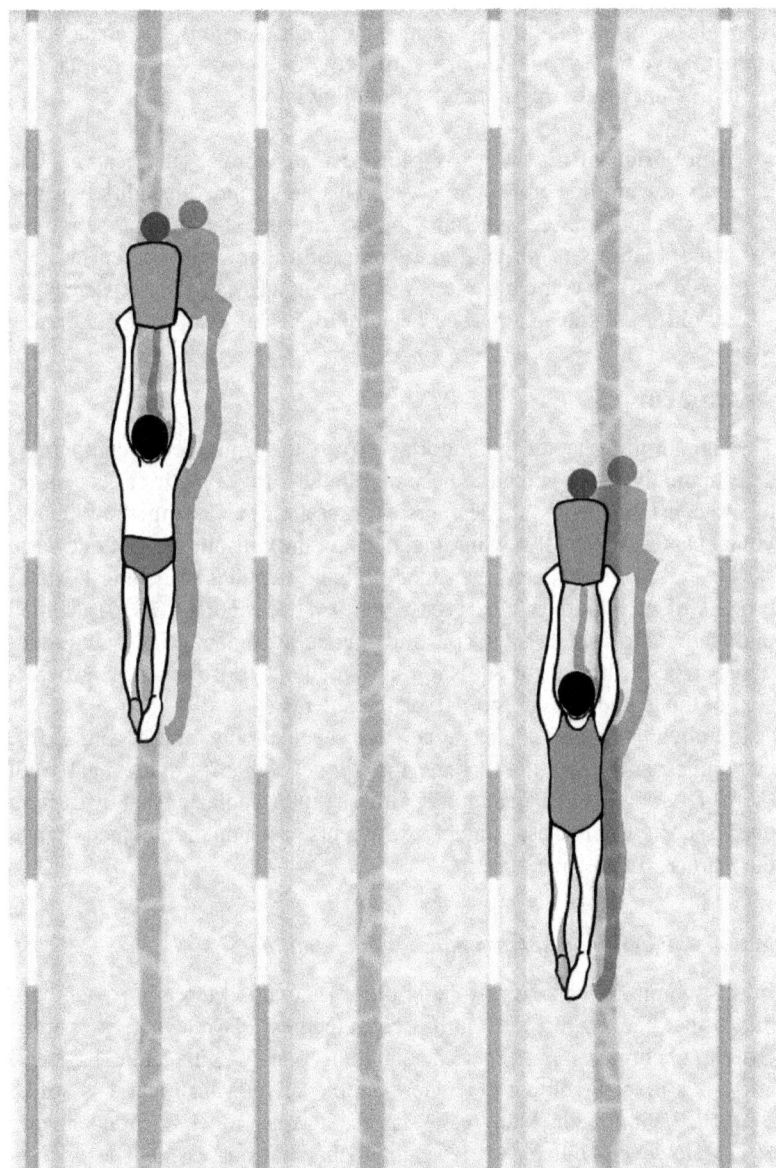

Figure 6.2 The objective of this game – to practice the flutter kick transporting a foam ball without touching it with a kickboard (permission provided by Ramon Friere).

Teaching adapted individual games through GCAs

Several examples on how to adapt swimming sessions for aquaphobic learners have been provided during the generic sessions. Other adaptations for individual games might include the following:

- **Simulation of different disabilities:** for example, have learners use only one arm/leg or using masks and learners' guide. In addition, learners can act as referees, helping their teammates start the competition.
- **Modifications of playing area and equipment:** cushion surfaces to avoid harm in combat games. Acoustics signals can also be used.
- **Avoiding obstacles:** this is especially for visually impaired children.

Assessment

Throughout this chapter the importance of both formative (or continuous) and summative assessment has been highlighted. Play practice asks instructors to constantly assess the learners' progression. This is important in individual games, especially swimming, because the consolidation of one basic skill (e.g., breathing) determines the following step in the teaching-learning process of a technique (e.g., breaststroke). Langendorfer (2015) claimed that there is a risk inherent in consolidating an inefficient habit by introducing specific techniques or skills too early without considering the progression of the learners using formative assessments.

In individual games contexts, there are specific tools for assessing skills, techniques and contexts such as the Model Athletic Assessment Tool (MAAT; Moore, 2017). In addition, Grosse (2005) indicated that instructors need to design ad hoc assessment instruments based on their objectives and the learners' needs and interests.

Motor skill development and games understanding

In the swimming context, Di Paola (2019) identified three important elements that can significantly influence outcomes: (1) relevant assessment criteria, (2) professional experience and observation skills and (3) systematic assessment methodology. One example of relevant criteria is stroke frequency and length (Madureira, Bastos, Corrêa, Rogel, & Freudenheim, 2012). However, Di Paola (2019) claimed that many assessment descriptors can make formative assessment difficult, especially among novice instructors. In contrast, he proposed acquiring a better understanding of the principles of movement in the water (i.e., hydrodynamics) as the key element to performance improvements, consistency or stability, persistence, level

Table 6.4 Crosstab proposed by Grosse (2005) to help coaches/teachers to effectively design comprehensive assessment tools for individual games/sports.

Assessment instruments	Decision-making	Skills	Knowledge	Behaviours	Attitudes
Teach backs	X	X	X	X	X
General checklists	X	X	X	X	X
Combined skill test	X	X	X		X
Scenarios	X		X		X
Journaling	X	X			X
Theoretical tests	X		X		X
Questionnaires			X	X	X
Interviews			X	X	X
Skill checklists	X	X			

of effort, attention and adaptability. Regarding observational skills, the use of slow-motion videos and technology (i.e., subaquatic cameras) can make assessment more effective.

Affective and social dimensions

Assessment does not only mean evaluating the proper execution of a specific technique (Karatrantou et al., 2019). Varveri et al. (2016) proposed the use of "friendly" assessment protocols to better evaluate personal levels of water competence (e.g., breathing control or underwater hearing; Langendorfer, 2015).

Grosse (2005) elaborated a crosstab (see Table 6.4) to link assessment tools with other areas of interest (i.e., behaviours or attitudes) that can be used to evaluate individual games/sports.

Swimming sessions are an ideal context to introduce aquatic rescue techniques and basic first aid concepts such as cardiopulmonary resuscitation (CPR). Although theoretical tests can be implemented to assess learners' knowledge, it is also important to evaluate their performance. Simulated situations (e.g., scenarios or role-playing) can help instructors observe and assess their learners' behaviour. Fleischhackl et al. (2009) recommend the use of a 13-item performance checklist grouped into three dimensions. Table 6.5 shows a model of this performance checklist.

Summary

Although individual games are mostly technical, tactical knowledge (i.e., decision-making) is also brought into the frame, and adequate progressions

Table 6.5 An emergency performance checklist based on Fleischhackl et al. (2009) applied in different simulated scenarios.

Scenario	You are a lifeguard in the swimming pool of your village. Suddenly, someone calls you because there is a man lying down in the showers. The man is unconscious. What do you do?		
Dimension	**Item**	**Yes**	**No**
Emergency call	They correctly dial the number of emergency services		
	They correctly detail the emergency, including the situation, the accident as well as the illness explanation		
	They correctly give the number of victims		
	They correctly detail the address of the emergency		
	They follow the instructions of the emergency operator or the doctor		
Vital signs	The responsiveness to stimuli is checked		
	They gently shake the patient (in the case that it is not a traffic accident or a violent impact to the ground)		
	They correctly call for help and give precise instructions		
	They open airways correctly		
	They check for normal breathing		
Recovery position	They put the victim into a stable recovery position (lateral position)		
	They remove any pressure on the victim's body		
	They open the airway sufficiently, directing the mouth downwards		

are important to promote learning. All learners must have opportunities for success and enjoyment, which are important in developing physically literate young people (Whitehead, 2010). Play Practice is a pedagogical model that can contribute to this important mission which emphasize the integration of tactics and techniques because "*What is tactically desirable must be technically possible*" (Launder & Piltz, 2013, p. 59). Challenges must be present during practice, and positive instructor feedback is essential to encourage learners. Throughout this chapter, the importance of conducting effective swimming assessment procedures has been emphasized and the most important assessment tools reviewed. In addition, the importance of integrating cross-sectional contexts (such as lifeguarding techniques), including the assessment periods, has been highlighted.

References

Adnan, M. W., Sedek, R., Mutalib, S. A., Kasim, Z. M., Kashim, M. I., Idris, F., & Yusof, A. (2019). Effects of swimming towards mental health in collegiate male adults. *Malaysian Applied Biology Journal, 48*(2), 141–148.

Almond, L. (1986). Reflecting on themes: a games classification. In R. D. Thorpe, D. J. Bunker, & L. Almond (Eds.), *Rethinking games teaching* (pp. 71–77). Loughborough: Department of Physical Education and Sports Sciences of the University of Loughborough.

American Red Cross (2014). *Water safety instructor's manual.* Morrisville, United States of America: Krames Stalywell Strategic Partnerships Division.

Baker, J., Yardley, J., & Côté, J. (2003). Coach behaviors and athlete satisfaction in team and individual sports. *International Journal of Sport Psychology, 34*(3), 226–239.

Batalla, A., & Martínez, P. (2002). *Deportes individuales* [Proposed English translation: *Individual sports*]. Barcelona, Spain: INDE Editorial.

Bouet, M. (1968). *Signification du sport* [Proposed English translation: *Meaning of sport*]. Paris, France: Editions Universitaires.

Di Paola, P. (2019). The assessment of swimming and survival skills: is your programme fit for its purpose? *International Journal of Aquatic Research and Education, 11*(4), 1–10. https://doi.org/10.25035/ijare.11.04.06

Dixon, H. E., & Bixler, R. D. (2007). Failure to learn to (really) swim: inflated self-efficacy? *Recreational Sports Journal, 31*(1), 14–20. https://doi.org/10.1123/rsj.31.1.14

Ellis, M. (1983). *Similarities and differences in games: a system for classification.* Conference Paper presented at International Association for Physical Education in Higher Education (AIESEP) Conference. Rome, Italy.

Famaey-Lamon, A., Hebbelinck, M., & Cadron, A. M. (1979). Team-sport and individual sport. *International Review of Sport Sociology, 14*(2), 37–50. https://doi.org/10.1177/101269027901400203

Fleischhackl, R., Nuernberger, A., Sterz, F., Schoenberg, C., Urso, T., Habart, T., . . . Chandra-Strobos, N. (2009). School children sufficiently apply life supporting first aid: a prospective investigation. *Critical Care, 13*(4), R127. https://doi.org/10.1186/cc7984

Goldsmith, W. (2015). Swimming 101: back to the basics. *Swimming World Magazine*, *3*, 30–31.

Grosse, S. J. (2005). Assessment of swimming in physical education. *Strategies*, *19*(1), 35–36. https://doi.org/10.1080/08924562.2005.11000388

International Swimming Federation (FINA) (2016). Swimming for all-swimming for life. *FINA Aquatics World Magazine*. Retrieved from www.fina.org/content/swimming-all-%E2%80%93-swimming-life

Karatrantou, K., Stavrou, V., Hasioti, P., Varveri, D., Krommidas, C., & Gerodimos, V. (2019). An enjoyable school-based swimming training programme improves students' aquaticity. *Acta Paediatrica*, *109*(1), 166–174. https://doi.org/10.1111/apa.14920

Langendorfer, S. J. (2015). Changing learn-to-swim and drowning prevention using aquatic readiness and water competence. *International Journal of Aquatic Research and Education*, *9*(1), 4–11. https://doi.org/10.25035/ijare.09.01.01

Launder, A. G. (2001). *Play Practice: the games approach to teaching and coaching sports*. Champaign, IL: Human Kinetics.

Launder, A. G., & Piltz, W. (2013). *Play Practice: engaging and developing skilled player from beginner to elite*. Champaign, IL: Human Kinetics.

Lazar, J. M., Khanna, N., Chesler, R., & Salciccioli, L. (2013). Swimming and the heart. *International Journal of Cardiology*, *168*(1), 19–26. https://doi.org/10.1016/j.ijcard.2013.03.063

Lee, J., & Kim, J. (2019). Development of survival swimming curriculum for prevention of drowning: delphi method. *Journal of Coastal Research*, *91*(1), 196–200. https://doi.org/10.2112/SI91-040.1

Madureira, F., Bastos, F. H., Corrêa, U. C., Rogel, T., & Freudenheim, A. M. (2012). Assessment of beginners' front-crawl stroke efficiency. *Perceptual & Motor Skills: Exercise & Sport*, *115*(1), 300–308. https://doi.org/10.2466/06.05.25.PMS.115.4.300-308

Mason, P. (2014). *Swim better, swim faster*. London: Bloomsbury.

Mische-Lawson, L., D'Adamo, J., Campbell, K., Hermreck, B., Holz, S., Moxley, J., . . . Travis, A. (2019). A qualitative investigation of swimming experiences of children with autism spectrum disorders and their families. *Clinical Medicine Insights: Pediatrics*, *13*(1), 1–9. https://doi.org/10.1177/1179556519872214

Moore, J. (2017). Model athletic assessment tool. *The Physical Educator*, *74*(1), 34–44. https://doi.org/10.18666/TPE-2017-V74-SI1-8551

Oliveira, D. V., Muzolon, L. G., Antunes, M. D., & Nascimento-Júnior, J. R. A. (2019). Impact of swimming initiation on the physical fitness and mental health of elderly women. *Acta Scientiarum. Health Sciences*, *41*(1), e43221. https://doi.org/10.4025/actascihealthsci.v41i1.43221

Siedentop, D., Hastie, P. A., & Van der Mars, H. (2020). *Complete guide to Sport Education* (3rd ed.). Champaign, IL: Human Kinetics.

Silverman, S. (1997). Is the tactical approach to teaching games better than a skills approach? *Journal of Physical Education, Recreation & Dance*, *68*(7), 5. https://doi.org/10.1080/07303084.1997.10604971

Szabo, A., Boros, S., Mezei, S., Németh, V., Soós, I., de la Vega, R., . . . Patakiné Bősze, J. (2019). Subjective psychological experiences in leisure and competitive swimming. *Annals of Leisure Research*, *22*(5), 629–641. https://doi.org/10.1080/11745398.2018.1558409

Varveri, D., Flouris, A. D., Smirnios, N., Pollatou, E., Karatzaferi, C., & Sakkas, G. K. (2016). Developing and testing an instrument to assess aquaticity in humans. *Journal of Bodywork and Movement Therapies*, *20*(3), 497–503. https://doi.org/10.1016/j.jbmt.2015.12.013

Vigário, P., Teixeira, A., & Mendes, F. (2020). Coach-athlete dyad: perception of psychosocial and environmental factors in the relationship-a case study. *Retos: Nuevas Tendencias en Educación Física, Deporte y Recreación*, *37*(1), 666–672.

Whitehead, M. (2010). *Physical literacy throughout the lifecourse*. Abingdon, Oxford: Routledge.

7 Future perspectives in Game-Centred Approaches
Hybridizations

Hybridizing pedagogical models

Alexander (2008) suggested that there has been a change in the conception of how to teach sports, from education "of" the physical to education "through" the physical (p. 3). In this sense, Hastie and Curnter-Smith (2006) noted that during the previous decades, there had been efforts to present models for teaching games that involve students participating in fair and equitable environments (places where all learners have opportunities for learning).

In the physical education context, as shown in Chapter 1 (p. 1), there has been a considerable interest in models-based practice (Casey, 2014; Metzler, 2017; Kirk, 2013). A model-based practice or pedagogical model is a way of organizing the interdependent elements of curriculum, learning and teaching to achieve specific learning outcomes (Hastie and Casey, 2014). It has been suggested that models-based practice seems to be the "bookies' favourite" (Casey, 2014, p. 19), and "a wave to the future" (Dyson, Griffin, & Hastie, 2004, p. 237) to replace traditional approaches.

However, it has also been acknowledged that one model is not capable of being effective in all contexts (Lund & Tannehill, 2010). As a possible solution, Stran, Sinelnikov and Woodruff (2012) noted that some researchers have attempted to fuse several curricular approaches in their teaching with the aim of using each model's beneficial features to achieve a particular purpose. This is possible because of some common features present in the models, such as the students' central role in the teaching process, the use of small-sided and conditioned games or the work in small groups.

These combinations produced the hybrid implementation of pedagogical models such as the Step-Game-Approach – Sport Education (SGA-SE) hybrid approach (Araújo, Hastie, Lohse, Bessa, & Mesquita, 2019) or the creation of new models such as the Sport for Peace Curriculum (Ennis, 1999), designed to enhance girls' levels of engagement and satisfaction, or

Empowering Sport (Hastie & Buchanan, 2000), a student-centred hybrid model focused on skill development, personal empowerment and social responsibility.

González-Víllora, Evangelio, Sierra-Díaz and Fernandez-Rio (2019) suggested that the term *hybridization* has been used to represent both ideas with the same starting point: "the combination of different pedagogical models or parts of them" (p. 1058). Other terms have been found in the literature to represent this hybridization/combination process, such as "mixing of models," "fusion," "marriage," "coalition," "integration of models" or "hybrid approaches." Regardless of the terminology used, the hybridizations can help increase the benefits and possibilities of individual pedagogical models (González-Víllora et al., 2019).

Hybridizing GCAs

Recently, González-Víllora et al. (2019) carried out a systematic review investigating the hybridizations conducted among pedagogical models in students from first to twelfth grade (six to 18 years) in the physical education context. They found an increased number of publications on this topic. Sport education (SE) was the most popularly used pedagogical model, and the combination SE-GCAs the most widely implemented, where Teaching Games for Understanding (TGfU) was the most highly used. The authors suggested that one plausible reason could be the adaptability and applicability of SE for teaching sports.

The focus of early implementations was to assess its viability, which led to the consideration of how these combinations could influence participants and their perceptions. However, although there is an evident proliferation of hybrid models in physical education, this is still scarce in extracurricular contexts.

The following sections provide an overview of the main results of current research, which has considered researchers, teachers, pre-service teachers and students' perceptions. Two main sections will be presented: hybridizations between GCAs and SE, and hybridizations between GCAs and cooperative learning (CL).

GCAs and SE

SE has been widely studied, and it is one of the most hybridized models. Hybrid models used the main characters of SE (formal competition with persisting teams or roles) with GCAs that focus more on specific pedagogies (Araújo, Mesquita, Hastie, & Pereira, 2016; Stran et al., 2012). When combined, these models can provide meaningful, purposeful and authentic learning activities for students (Dyson et al., 2004). In addition, these hybrid approaches do not undermine the advantages of each model but use the strengths of each to ease specific gaps in each of them (Mesquita, Farias, & Hastie, 2012).

In this section, we would like to highlight the Portuguese contribution to this field, which aimed to consider the specificity of tactics within different sports (e.g., invasion games or net/wall games) and have opened a new line in the study of hybrid models with specific sports' tactics.

The following sections are grouped by the type of hybridization used (e.g., TGfU-SE and TGA-SE).

TGfU-SE

TGfU and SE were developed in the 1980s, when new thinking emerged on how to effectively teach sport (Alexander, 2008). Both pedagogical models aimed to provide students with the opportunity to participate in modified games (Bunker & Thorpe, 1982; Siedentop, 1994). Hastie and Curnter-Smith (2006) noted that the combination of TGfU and SE had the potential to promote game understanding and affective goals.

In addition, Stran et al. (2012) suggested that SE and TGfU seemed to complement each other because both share the intention of shifting responsibility from the teacher to the learners. From a practical perspective, this hybridization allows SE to run as intended but enhance game play focusing on tactical problems (Stran et al., 2012). Furthermore, Alexander (2008) advised that, although it is claimed that TGfU situates learning within authentic contexts, TGfU cannot be fully authentic if the characteristics that Siedentop (1994) assigns to SE are not used. Although these models have different foci, there is a logical coalition between them, given that both models provide sport experiences which help students learn how to play well (Hastie & Curnter-Smith, 2006).

Research seems to suggest that fusing SE with TGfU would allow instructors to benefit from the structural guidance (what is to be taught: SE) and support (how to go about it: TGfU) (Alexander & Penney, 2005). However, the challenge in a TGfU-SE combination is to develop effective teaching strategies to support student-mediated instructional activity without compromising the "student-centredness" of SE (Alexander & Penney, 2005, p. 291).

Hastie and Curnter-Smith (2006) examined the influence of a hybrid TGfU-SE unit of batting/fielding games on elementary school students and their teachers, with positive results for student enjoyment and appreciation of the affiliation provided by SE; although this same feature also provided negative experiences (e.g., team selection). Students were able to provide correct responses to tactical questions and perceived positive improvements in their game related skills. These results seemed to indicate that students' tactical ability improved during the course of the unit. These authors emphasized that the combination of these models did not weaken the structural advantages that research has suggested SE has over traditional approaches. However, modifications had to be made on both models to make them compatible with each other. In this sense, they suggested that instructional and managerial tasks associated with both models take time, and it is recommended that each model be practiced and mastered before they are combined.

Some years later, Stran et al. (2012) examined pre-service teachers' perceptions of teaching a TGfU-SE invasion games hybrid unit with fifth-grade students. Pre-service teachers indicated that both models connected and were beneficial to students' engagement in the season, reporting that students had fun and used strategies and tactics, with gains in confidence and success. A few pre-service teachers saw limitations when implementing each individual model, but they saw the combination positive, acknowledging their experience with both models separately when implementing the hybrid model. However, some pre-service teachers noted the difficulty of implementing the mixing of models. For example, they had trouble with some SE characteristics (e.g., pre-season games were unorganized) or those of TGfU (e.g., during questioning pre-service teachers answered the question to give a fast response to students).

Recent interventions in the Spanish context have also provided positive results from this combination. Gil-Arias, Harvey, Cárceles, Práxedes and Del Villar (2017) showed improvements in autonomy, competence, enjoyment and the intention to be physically active in TGfU-SE volleyball and ultimate Frisbee in tenth-grade students. Antón-Candanedo and Fernandez-Rio (2017) went a step further in TGfU-SE research and included homemade materials in the learning unit for tenth-grade students using an alternative sport (Duni). The students, particularly the girls, suggested tactical improvements. More recently, Gil-Arias, Claver, Práxedes, Villar and Harvey (2020) evaluated autonomy support, perceived motivational climate, enjoyment and perceived competence in a hybrid TGfU-SE in comparison with a unit delivered via direct instruction in fourth year secondary education students, obtaining higher scores for the hybrid TGfU-SE unit.

TGA-SE (the Sport Education Tactical Model [SETM])

In 2009, Pritchard and McCollum proposed the Sport Education Tactical Model (SETM), connecting SE and the Tactical Games Approach (TGA), with the same aims as SE: to develop *competent, literate* and *enthusiastic* sportspersons (Siedentop, Hastie and Van der Mars, 2020).

Gubacs-Collins and Olsen (2010) discussed the challenges faced by a middle school practitioner over a five-year period when implementing TGA with SE in elementary school students. The teacher found the implementation of tactical models challenging; although he suggested that SE combined with TGA provided opportunities to improve the way in which sports are taught. He believed that it could be helpful to implement SE and TGA concurrently rather than in isolation because SE's features provide the organizational structure necessary to implement TGA. This idea clashed with previous scholars who had recommended SE and TGA to be implemented separately before they are combined (Collier, 2005).

A few years later, Pritchard, McCollum, Sundal and Colquit (2014) investigated the effectiveness of SETM using basketball in middle school physical education, with positive results in game performance for girls and boys. The authors suggested that features of SETM (e.g., longer units or affiliation) led to improvements in game performance, providing time for students to play games and understand them.

Invasion Games Competence Model (IGCM)-SE

Farias, Mesquita and Hastie (2019) believed that developing competent game players is complex, especially in invasion games. In this respect, Mesquita et al. (2012) suggested that TGfU does not consider the specificity of tactics within team sports, which makes it necessary to address it through specific models, such as the IGCM, which adapts TGfU features to invasion games (e.g., tactical principles).

Mesquita et al. (2012) examined the impact of the application of a hybrid IGCM-SE on fifth-grade students' game performance during a soccer intervention. The learning task structure provided by IGCM offered students the opportunity to improve their skill execution and decision-making, especially with girls and lower-skilled students. Similar results were found in Farias, Mesquita and Hastie's (2015) study, who used the same sport and same-grade students. These studies suggested that females seemed to take greater advantage of the implemented programme than males.

Some years later, Farias, Mesquita, Hastie and O'Donovan (2018), in a longitudinal study, examined the impact of three consecutive IGCM-SE seasons on seventh-grade students playing basketball, handball and soccer. This study aimed to understand how student-coaches perform their roles in SE. The results supported the potential of SE to develop players and the importance of prolonged interventions to enhance tactical understanding and concluded that, with adequate preparation of specific strategies, student-coaches were able to provide feedback to their partners and adjust game conditions during the game. In a similar research program, Farias et al. (2019) showed that the game performance index increased progressively across seasons in seventh-grade students experiencing three consecutive hybrid seasons, primarily due to the extended team membership, peer-teaching mediation and game forms design.

SGA-SE

SGA could have the potential to provide an appropriate framework for the development of game performance in net/wall sports (e.g., volleyball or badminton) (Mesquita, Graça, Gomes, & Cruz, 2005). SGA is based on the step-by-step presentation of game problems that challenge players' capacity to understand the game (Mesquita et al., 2005).

Araújo, Mequita, Hastie, Farias and Santos (2013) analyzed the evolution of content knowledge from the teacher to student-coaches on a SGA-SE hybrid unit in seventh-grade students. The results showed difficulties for student-coaches to understand the aims of the tasks. However, some years later, Araújo, Hastie, Pereira and Mesquita (2017) examined the evolution of student-coaches' pedagogical content knowledge during three hybrid SGA-SE seasons in volleyball over three years (students from seventh to ninth grade). Developing specific protocols, the authors highlighted that it was possible for student-coaches to organize and present tasks to their teammates, to identify skill errors and provide feedback, and to show the ability to adapt tasks for team members. Despite SE being a student-centred approach, the authors noted that giving students complete autonomy is not an easy task, and it is necessary to shift responsibility gradually to them.

Regarding game performance within this hybridization, Araújo et al. (2016) examined seventh-grade students practicing volleyball, with positive results in almost all the indexes evaluated. Later, Araújo et al. (2019) analyzed students' volleyball game play performance improvements across three hybrid SGA-SE seasons during three years. Students made improvements from pre- to post-test during each season, the low-skilled being those with major improvements. The authors of both studies suggested that the hybrid SGA-SE season could have the potential to enhance game play development and, at the same time, facilitate SE's affective and social goals.

GCAs and CL

In their article about possible combinations between pedagogical models, Dyson et al. (2004) suggested that tactical approaches and cooperative learning (CL) could be combined to improve learning environments.

TGA-CL

Casey and Dyson (2009) combined CL and TGA to teach tennis to seventh-grade boys. The authors showed the worries and difficulties that a teacher can face when combining these two models, summarized as (1) planning as a difficult endeavour; (2) difficulties when changing the teacher role within the lessons (to a more student-centred environment); and (3) organization. At first there were problems with cooperation and interaction among students, but this environment changed to a more organized and cooperative one (i.e., students helped those players who needed more). Additionally, there was a positive evolution in the students' skill levels. The teacher suggested that the difficulties for students were not so much the TGA but the inherent structures in the cooperative approach. However, the authors suggested that combining these models has advantages for students and teachers. Later, Casey and MacPhail (2018) also reported positive results when implementing a hybrid TGA-CL (joined to other models) with seventh-grade boys, showing positive results in students' engagement and responsibility. They suggested that previous experience with the models and sufficient time helped in the implementation. Definitely, as it is show in Figure 7.1.,

Figure 7.1 Learners' suggestions in TGA-CL join as a "puzzle" for developing values and common goals (permission provided by Ramon Friere).

a hybridization should be considered as a giant puzzle of critical elements that enhace the holistic development of everybody.

GCA hybridizations main conclusions

Research in hybrid GCAs models suggest that they are gaining more recognition in physical education contexts. Unfortunately, there is no research in extracurricular sport. Despite this growing interest in hybridizing GCAs with SE or CL, there is a lack of hybrid GCA implementations with other consolidated pedagogical models (Fernandez-Rio, Hortigüela, & Pérez-Pueyo, 2018), such as Teaching Personal and Social Responsibility. In addition, there is no research that has examined the impact of a hybrid GCA with what Fernandez-Rio et al. (2018) call emergent models (e.g., Adventure Education or Health-Based Physical Education).

The main conclusions of GCA hybrid implementations are presented as follows:

- Teachers implementing these hybrids can experience difficulties (the change to a student-centred environment).
- Instructional and managerial tasks associated with these hybridizations take time and patience, particularly if the teachers and/or the students have not previously experienced student-centred models. Generally, it is suggested that each model be practiced and mastered in isolation before combining them.
- Research supports these coalitions with positive outcomes in game performance, engagement, fun and confidence.
- Different results have been achieved in relation to gender or skill level.

Fidelity protocols

Why verify implementation?

Hastie and Casey (2014) presented a document to guide reporting of future research using pedagogical models. They suggested that each model has a specific design that prescribes the "non-negotiable features that make it distinctive" (p. 422). Metzler (2017) alluded to these non-negotiable features as benchmarks.

Hastie and Casey (2014) acknowledged the flexibility of each model, which allows teachers, coaches or researchers to design units that are adapted to specific contexts. However, they also suggested that some form of fidelity of implementation should be reported to verify that the features of the models have been correctly used.

How to verify implementation

Hastie and Casey (2014) proposed three key elements that are essential in any research design:

- **Rich description of the curricular elements of the unit:** a clear description of the intervention is needed to identify how the non-negotiable aspects of the model have been included.
- **Detailed validation of model implementation:** validation is needed to ensure that the instruction was consistent with the accepted standards of the model.
- **Detailed description of the programme context:** failure to report important contextual details can result in wrong conclusions being drawn. Some critical aspects that must be reported are teacher/coach and learners' previous experience with a particular model, instructional time (e.g., number of lessons, length of these lessons or number of lessons conducted each week) and facilitators and constraints (e.g., student groupings, weather or equipment).

Table 7.1 provides some examples of benchmarks, checklists and full descriptions that will help the reader validate future implementations.

Hybridizing TGA and SE: considerations and practical application in tennis

It is difficult to provide details of how a hybrid model works. One reason is that each variation or small modification in the implementation of the main features of the models may result in important changes in the hybridization. Nevertheless, this section will suggest some ideas that those who want to combine pedagogical models should consider.

What are teachers going to teach and how?

This section is not only based on the content teachers want to teach, in this case, tennis, but also the tactical level they want to develop based on the starting level of the students. In this sense, Hastie and Curnter-Smith (2006) considered that it was imperative for instructors to be knowledgeable on the content they are going to teach. The learning outcomes need to be clearly defined, whether they are cognitive, physical, social or affective. All these decisions will be determined by the characteristics of the learners. This example is based on a tennis mixed-gender club (extracurricular sport) with 16 players.

Table 7.1 Tools for verifying hybrid GCA implementation.

Hybridization	Examples of recommended references
Hybridization GCA-SEs (general):	
SE	• Metzler (2017, pp. 282–283) – SE teacher and student benchmarks. • Sinelnikov (2009, p. 100) – benchmarks. • Stran et al. (2012, p. 293) – benchmarks. • Hastie et al. (2013, p. 339) – instructional checklist (SE and traditional approach).
GCAs	• Stran et al. (2012, p. 294) – tactical games teacher benchmarks. • Metzler (2017, pp. 376–377) – TGA teacher and student benchmarks. • Butler (2014, pp. 13–15) – benchmarks for TGfU beliefs, intentions and actions.
Other hybridizations:	
TGfU-SE	• Gil-Arias et al. (2017, p. 8) – instructional checklist.
TGA-SE (SETM)	• Pritchard and McCollum (2009, pp. 32–37) – practical description. • Gubacs-Collins and Olsen (2010, pp. 40–41) – practical description.
IGCM-SE	• Farias et al. (2015) – complete season plan description. • Mesquita et al. (2012) – complete season plan description.
SGA-SE	• Araújo et al. (2016, p. 191) – instructional checklist. • Araújo et al. (2019, p. 317) – instructional checklist.
TGA-CL	• Metzler (2017, pp. 249–250) – CL teacher and student benchmarks.

What features of each model should be maintained?

It is important to bear in mind the main characteristics of each model to maintain the nature of the models. However, sometimes these have to be adapted to both models for them to complement each other.

TGA

Based on a particular tactical problem (e.g., winning the point), a decision must be made as to how best to solve it during the session. Modified games and practice tasks are used to develop learners' game performance.

SE

The season will be made up of 20 sessions, divided into three phases: pre-season (including friendly matches), formal competition and a culminating event (in this case a tournament against another tennis club). The players will remain on the same team (mixed, skill-level balanced) during the entire season and will perform different roles (i.e., player-coach, conditioning coach, equipment manager, captain and referee). There will be an official schedule to ensure equitable participation for all teams, which will be single and double format in tennis. Each game in this competition phase will last 10 minutes to make sure that the timetable for each session is completed. Throughout the season, data on several elements is kept (e.g., best play, fair play, effort, etc.). The season will be framed by a festive environment. In this chapter, "coach" will refer to the adult, and "player-coach" will mean the learner.

Hybridizing the models

As suggested by Alexander and Penney (2005), this kind of hybridization will include both coach-mediated (active and task teaching and teaching through questions) and player-mediated strategies (peer tutoring, reciprocal teaching or small-group/cooperative learning). The structure recommended by González-Víllora, Evangelio, Guijarro and Rocamora (2020) to hybridize SE and a tactical model was followed using important strategies for building tactical knowledge:

Strategies for building tactical knowledge:

- **Questioning** (see Pearson & Webb, 2008): the coach will meet with the whole group or with each team for questioning after the games are played to build tactical knowledge.
- **Dossier of games:** teams will receive a dossier of games, which will include instructions and drawings of the games and error detection to help players give feedback to their partners.
- **Coaches' corner:** When new content is introduced, the coach will provide the key points of the tasks and content to be taught to the player-coach, while the rest of the learners continue their practice. This is referred as "coaches' corner strategy" by Araújo et al. (2017).
- **Half-time period:** during the 10-minute games (competition phase), there will be a half-time period (at minute five) when players can reflect on tactical questions from the first period.
- **Tactical time-out** (Harvey, Cope, & Jones, 2016): the captain may call for a tactical time-out during the games. The players can request the player-coach's assistance to help them identify tactical or technical problems (see Figure 7.2).

Future perspectives in GCAs 123

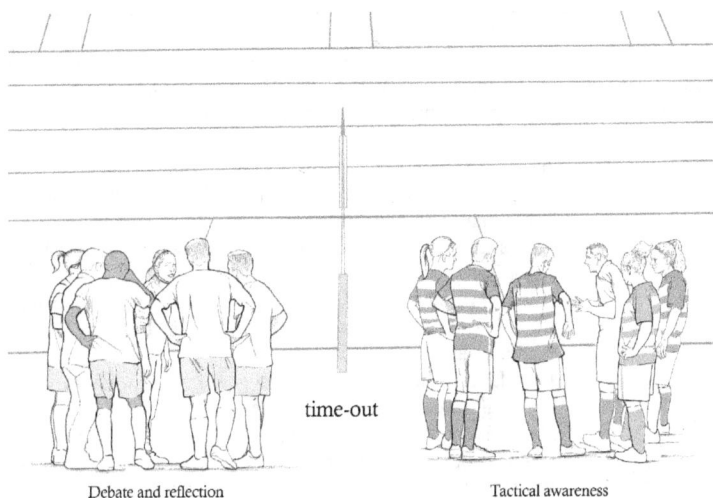

Figure 7.2 Tactical time-out on TGA-SE (permission provided by Ramon Friere).

Pre-season within the hybrid TGA-SE

During the first sessions in the pre-season, the coach will introduce the main characteristics of SE. Initial sessions will involve coach direction and, as the season progresses, they will give more responsibility to the learners, using more indirect teaching strategies (i.e., guided discovery) and showing player-coaches how to teach their own games. When necessary, the coach can intervene to introduce techniques or tactics.

Learners will participate in small-sided games, first guided by the teacher through questions to understand tactics and strategies. The learners performing their roles will lead their warm-ups, team practices and friendly matches. At first, the player-coach will lead the instruction of simpler tasks and as the season progresses will lead more complex learning tasks based on their team game problems. During the first sessions, the coach can provide short demonstrations of the games or tasks to the whole group, and when player-coaches gain confidence performing their role, the coach can provide short demonstrations of the games or tasks to the player-coaches who will show them to their team.

Table 7.2 provides an example of a typical session in the middle of the pre-season. Before the session begins, the player-coaches and the coach will meet to discuss the tactical problems that might arise in the session

Table 7.2 A typical day during pre-season.

Time	Activities conducted
10'–15' (before the session)	Player-coaches and coach meeting: discuss and debate about tactical problems and possible solutions.
5'	Physical trainer: consult the dossier of games to prepare the explanation of the game and list the equipment responsibility and material necessary.
	Equipment responsibility: collect the necessary material for the session.
15'	Physical trainer: leads the warm-up in the teams' home area.
10'	Whole group tactical awareness led by the coach.
15'	Practice task.
15'	The player-coaches lead the final game in the session.
5'	Physical trainer leads the stretches.
15'	Flag design: teams' affiliation.
10'	Whole group final meeting.

(e.g., winning the point) and possible solutions to those problems (10–15 minutes in duration). The session begins when the players enter the gym and go to their home areas. Once the four members of the team are in their home areas, the player-coach will take a look at the dossier of games and will tell the equipment manager what is needed. At the same time, the conditioning coach will explain the game. They will lead a singles game in which the goal is to win the point attacking the net, played to four points. The player-coach will use the dossier of games to explain the main aspects of the game (e.g., punctuation, space, material). While all the teams are playing, the coach will monitor practice, giving feedback and observing the tactical or technical problems the four teams are experiencing.

After approximately 15 minutes, the whole group will meet to discuss the problems they are facing playing the games. The coach will ask questions such as "What should be done in this situation?" or "What did you do after a short ground stroke?" Then, the coach will explain a practice task that all teams will perform in their court areas based on the tactical and technical problems the players and coach have highlighted (e.g., land four to six approach shots in the backcourt). Finally, the coach will introduce the final game (after explaining it to the player-coaches in the meeting before the session). This game will be more complex than the first one to use the concepts learnt. The equipment manager will collect the material and return it to the storage room.

The conditioning coach will lead the stretches, and then the team members will continue designing their flag for the formal competition. The equipment manager will keep the flag, and the captain will make sure that a fair play environment is kept, managing any conflict that may arise. If necessary, they will ask the coach for a solution. Then, a whole-group final meeting will be held during which all teams and the coach will talk about the session.

Formal competition within the hybrid TGA-SE

Table 7.3 presents a typical sports day during formal competition. The players enter the gym and immediately check the match schedule on the wall of the gymnasium. All the members of each team meet in their assigned home courts to decide on the game (from five possible games in the dossier) to begin their practice, selecting one to reinforce the tactical or technical problems previously observed. Once the game has been chosen, the equipment manager collects the necessary material, and the four members of the team begin to play. Before the end of the game, the coach will meet with the person performing the referee role in each group to coordinate their tasks during the matches.

After an agreed time, the teams go to the starting point in the gym for the parade. When it is over, the competition starts (using the previously agreed schedule). Each match will last 10 minutes, with a half-time break of 1 minute. The games will be singles or doubles, following the schedule. Each team will have the opportunity to ask for a team-out, when they can join with the teammates and discuss the problems they are having during the match. They can also consult the coach. The referees will time and register the results. The teams that are not playing at this point are required to train, and they can ask for coach support to play the best game for them (based on the games' dossier), reviewing some of the tactical problems they had during previous matches. The coach can guide the selection process,

Table 7.3 A typical day during formal competition.

Time	Activities conducted
10'	Players' meeting for selecting the game based on the final meeting in the last session.
15'	The players play the decided game.
10'	Teams' parade.
40'	Competition. Teams will play games against other teams. Teams will referee. Teams will train.
5'	The physical trainer leads stretches.
10'	Final meeting and referees' evaluation.

attending to the teams' demands and, once the game has been chosen, will provide guided discovery. Players can also design their own game based on the knowledge they acquired during the formal competition.

At the end of the competition, teams return to their home areas, referees announce the scores and the coach assigns fair play points or best team points and notes them on the leader board located in a visible place (e.g., the gymnasium wall). The conditioning coach will run the stretches, and all the players will go to the starting point for the final group meeting, where teams will discuss the refereeing and the whole session.

Culminating event within the hybrid TGA-SE

During the final phase, teams will compete against other club teams in a festive environment. Individuals will continue performing their roles (e.g., referee, player-coach, etc.).

Evaluation and assessment

Validation: evaluation of the intervention

As previously noted, each intervention should be validated. Metzler's benchmarks (2017), or Pritchard and McCollum (2009) and the practical descriptions of Gubacs-Collins and Olsen (2010) could be useful tools.

Assessment: learners' evaluations

Tactical development, skill performance, effort, responsibility and role performance are some elements that should be evaluated. Sections in the previous practical chapters can guide coaches/teachers to adapt the instruments introduced.

Summary

This chapter introduces the existing literature on hybrid GCA models, reviewing their viability for young learners and providing examples of how to implement them. Finally, some validation procedures are included to help future implementations.

References

Alexander, K. (2008). Is there a role for tactical and Sport Education Models in school physical education? In *First Asia Pacific Sport in Education Conference*. Adelaide, Australia.

Alexander, K., & Penney, D. (2005). Teaching under the influence: Feeding Games for Understanding into the Sport Education development-refinement cycle. *Physical Education and Sport Pedagogy*, *10*(3), 287–301. https://doi.org/10.1080/17408980500340901

Antón-Candanedo, A., & Fernandez-Rio, J. (2017). Hibridando modelos pedagógicos para la mejora de la comprensión táctica de estudiantes: una investigación a través del Duni [Hybridizing pedagogical models for the improvement of students' tactical understanding: an investigation through Duni]. *Ágora para la Educación Física y el Deporte*, *19*(2–3), 257–276. https://doi.org/10.24197/aefd.2-3.2017.257-276

Araújo, R., Hastie, P., Lohse, K. R., Bessa, C., & Mesquita, I. (2019). The long-term development of volleyball game play performance using Sport Education and the Step-Game-Approach model. *European Physical Education Review*, *25*(2), 311–326. https://doi.org/10.1177/1356336X17730307

Araújo, R., Hastie, P. A., Pereira, C. & Mesquita, I. (2017). The evolution of student-coach's pedagogical content knowledge in a combined use of Sport Education and the Step-Game-Approach model. *Physical Education and Sport Pedagogy*, *22*(5), 518–535. https://doi.org/10.1080/17408989.2017.1294668

Araújo, R., Mequita, I., Hastie, P. A., Farias, C., & Santos, D. (2013). Content knowledge of the student-coach in peer teaching tasks in a hybrid SE-SGA volleyball unit. *Revista Mineira de Educaçao Física*, *9*(1), 49–55.

Araújo, R., Mesquita, I., Hastie, P., & Pereira, C. (2016). Students' game performance improvements during a hybrid Sport Education-Step-Game-Approach volleyball unit. *European Physical Education Review*, *22*(2), 185–200. https://doi.org/10.1177/1356336X15597927

Bunker, D., & Thorpe, R. (1982). A model for the teaching of games in secondary schools. *Bulletin of Physical Education*, *18*(1), 5–8.

Butler, J. (2014). TGfU – Would you know it if you saw it? Benchmarks from the tacit knowledge of the founders. *European Physical Education Review*, *20*(4), 465–488. https://doi.org/10.1177/1356336X14534356

Casey, A. (2014). Models-Based Practice: great white hope or white elephant? *Physical Education & Sport Pedagogy*, *19*(1), 18–34. https://doi.org/10.1080/17408989.2012.726977

Casey, A., & Dyson, B. (2009). The implementation of Models-Based Practice in physical education through action research. *European Physical Education Review*, *15*(2), 175–199. https://doi.org/10.1177/1356336X09345222

Casey, A., & MacPhail, A. (2018). Adopting a models-based approach to teaching physical education. *Physical Education & Sport Pedagogy*, *23*(3), 294–310. https://doi.org/10.1080/17408989.2018.1429588

Collier, C. S. (2005). Integrating Tactical Games and Sport Education models. In L. L. Griffin & J. I. Butler (Eds.), *Teaching Games for Understanding: theory, research, and practice* (pp. 137–148). Champaign, IL: Human Kinetics.

Dyson, B., Griffin, L., & Hastie, P. A. (2004). Sport education, tactical games, and cooperative learning: Theoretical and pedagogical considerations. *Quest*, *56*(2), 226–240. https://doi.org/10.1080/00336297.2004.10491823

Ennis, C. D. (1999). Creating a culturally relevant curriculum for disengaged girls. *Sport, Education and Society*, *4*(1), 31–49. https://doi.org/10.1080/1357332990 040103

Farias, C., Mesquita, I., & Hastie, P. A. (2015). Game performance and understanding within a hybrid Sport Education season. *Journal of Teaching in Physical Education*, *34*(3), 363–388. https://doi.org/10.1123/jtpe.2013-0149

Farias, C., Mesquita, I., & Hastie, P. A. (2019). Student game-play performance in invasion games following three consecutive hybrid Sport Education seasons. *European Physical Education Review*, *25*(3), 691–712. https://doi.org/10. 1177/1356336X18769220

Farias, C., Mesquita, I., Hastie, P. A., & O'Donovan, T. (2018). Mediating peer teaching for learning games: an action research intervention across three consecutive Sport Education seasons. *Research Quarterly for Exercise and Sport*, *89*(1), 91–102. https://doi.org/10.1080/02701367.2017.1402114

Fernandez-Rio, J., Hortigüela, D., & Pérez-Pueyo, A. (2018). Revisando los modelos pedagógicos en educación física. Ideas clave para incorporarlos al aula [Reviewing the pedagogical models in Physical Education. Keynotes for incorporating them into the classroom]. *Revista Española de Educación Física y Deportes*, *423*, 57–80.

Gil-Arias, A., Claver, F., Práxedes, A., Villar, F. D., & Harvey, S. (2020). Autonomy support, motivational climate, enjoyment and perceived competence in physical education: impact of a hybrid Teaching Games for Understanding/Sport Education unit. *European Physical Education Review*, *26*(1), 36–53. https://doi. org/10.1177/1356336X18816997

Gil-Arias, A., Harvey, S., Cárceles, A., Práxedes, A., & Del Villar, F. (2017). Impact of a hybrid TGfU-Sport Education unit on student motivation in physical education. *PLoS ONE*, *12*(6), e0179876. https://doi.org/10.1371/journal.pone.0179876

González-Víllora, S., Evangelio, C., Guijarro, E., & Rocamora, I. (2020). *Innovando con el modelo de Educación Deportiva: si buscas resultados distintos, no eduques de la misma manera* [Proposed English translation: *Innovating with the Sports Education model: if you are looking for different results, do not educate in the same way*]. Aula Magna: McGraw Hill.

González-Víllora, S., Evangelio, C., Sierra-Díaz, J., & Fernandez-Rio, J. (2019). Hybridizing pedagogical models: a systematic review. *European Physical Education Review*, *25*(4), 1056–1074. https://doi.org/10.1177%2F1356336X18797363

Gubacs-Collins, K., & Olsen, E. B. (2010). Implementing a Tactical Games Approach with Sport Education. A chronicle. *Journal of Physical Education, Recreation & Dance*, *81*(3), 36–42. https://doi.org/10.1080/07303084.2010.10598447

Harvey, S., Cope, E., & Jones, T. (2016). Developing questioning in Game-Centered Approaches. *Journal of Physical Education, Recreation & Dance*, *87*(3), 28–35. doi:10.1080/07303084.2015.1131212

Hastie, P. A., & Buchanan, A. M. (2000). Teaching responsibility through Sport Education: prospects of a coalition. *Research Quarterly for Exercise and Sport*, *71*(1), 25–35. https://doi.org/10.1080/02701367.2000.10608877

Hastie, P.A., Calderón, A., Rolim, R. J., & Guarino, A. J. (2013). The development of skill and knowledge during a Sport Education season of track and field athletics. Research Quarterly for Exercise and Sport, 84(3), 336–344. https://doi.org/10.1080/02701367.2013.812001

Hastie, P. A., & Casey, A. (2014). Fidelity in Models-Based Practice research in sport pedagogy: a guide for future investigations. *Journal of Teaching in Physical Education*, 33(3), 422–431. https://doi.org/10.1123/jtpe.2013-0141

Hastie, P. A., & Curnter-Smith, M. D. (2006). Influence of a hybrid Sport Education – Teaching Games for Understanding unit on one teacher and his students. *Physical Education & Sport Pedagogy*, 11(1), 1–27. https://doi.org/10.1080/17408980500466813

Kirk, D. (2013). Educational value and Models-Based Practice in physical education. *Educational Philosophy and Theory*, 45(9), 973–986. https://doi.org/10.1080/00131857.2013.785352

Lund, J., & Tannehill, D. (2010). *Standards-based physical education curriculum development* (2nd ed.). Sudbury, ON: Jones and Bartlett Publishers.

Mesquita, I., Farias, C., & Hastie, P. A. (2012). The impact of a hybrid Sport Education – Invasion Games Competence Model soccer unit on students' decision making, skill execution and overall game performance. *European Physical Education Review*, 18(2), 205–219. https://doi.org/10.1177/1356336X12440027

Mesquita, I., Graça, A., Gomes, A. R., & Cruz, C. (2005). Examining the impact of a Step Game Approach to teaching volleyball on student tactical decision making and skill execution during game play. *Journal of Human Movement Studies*, 48(6), 469–492. https://doi.org/10.1177/1356336X12440027

Metzler, M. (2017). *Instructional models for physical education* (3rd ed.). New York: Routledge-Falmer.

Pearson, P. J., & Webb, P. (2008). Developing effective questioning in Teaching Games for Understanding (TGfU). Conference Paper presented at *First Asia Pacific Sport in Education Conference*. Adelaide, Australia.

Pritchard, T., & McCollum, S. (2009). The Sport Education Tactical Model. *Journal of Physical Education, Recreation & Dance*, 80(9), 31–38. https://doi.org/10.1080/07303084.2009.10598392

Pritchard, T., McCollum, S., Sundal, J., & Colquit, G. (2014). Effect of the Sport Education Tactical Model on coeducational and single gender game performance. *The Physical Educator*, 71(1), 132–154.

Siedentop, D. (1994). *Sport Education: quality PE through positive sport experiences*. Champaign, IL: Human Kinetics.

Siedentop, D., Hastie, P. A., & van der Mars, H. (2020). *Complete guide to Sport Education* (3rd ed.). Champaign, IL: Human Kinetics.

Sinelnikov, O. A. (2009). Sport Education for teachers: professional development when introducing a novel curriculum model. *European Physical Education Review*, 15(1), 91–114. https://doi.org/10.1177/1356336x09105213

Stran, M., Sinelnikov, O., & Woodruff, E. (2012). Pre-service teachers' experiences implementing a hybrid curriculum: Sport Education and Teaching Games for Understanding. *European Physical Education Review*, 18(3), 287–308. https://doi.org/10.1177/1356336X12450789

Analytical index

Note: The practical applications are listed in **bold**.

abki 73
active lifestyle 1, 9, 10
active reflection 4, 5, 7, 11, 12, 97, 122
adaptation (of games) 6, 13, 25, 41, 54, 58, 59, 66, 74, 94, 100, 106
adapted sport(s) 36, 37, 54
adjustment index 88
adventure education 119
affective dimension 107
aquaphobia 100, 106
aquatic environment 97, 101, 103
aquatic rescue technique 101, 107
archery 72, 75
assessment instrument(s) 36, 54, 68, 86, 106, 107
athlete(s) 2, 3, 4, 5, 8, 12, 62, 63, 65, 68, 79, 81, 82, 83, 87, 92, 94
athlete-centred approach 3
athletics 6, 92, 93
attacker(s) 27, 31, 32, 34, 35, 59, 60
attack the goal 24, 29, 30, 31
Attitudes to Moral Decision-Making in Youth Sport Questionnaire 88
authentic 2, 14, 24, 113, 114
authentic assessment 14
autism spectrum disorder 97
autonomy 115, 117
avoid progression 24, 34
avoid the goal 24

badminton 6, 8, 40, 41, 42, 45, 54, 55
ball(s) 11, 13, 23, 24, 25, 26, 27, 28, 29, 30, 31, 32, 33, 34, 35, 36, 37, 40, 41, 42, 44, 45, 54, 58, 59, 60, 61, 62, 63, 64, 65, 66, 67, 68, 69, 72, 73, 75, 76, 79, 80, 81, 82, 83, 84, 85, 86, 87, 92, 93, 95, 100, 102, 103, 104, 105, 115, 116, 117
ball sports 92, 93
barricades 77
baseball 6, 58, 61, 62
basketball 6, 13, 23, 24, 26, 36, 42, 80, 116
batting and fielding games 58
behaviour 1, 10, 11, 15, 36, 70, 86, 92, 102, 107
benchmark 119, 120, 121, 126
billiards 72
blueprint 7
bocce 72
boccia 78
bowling 6, 72, 79, 80, 81, 82
breath 97, 98, 99, 102, 103, 104, 106, 107, 108
British bulldogs 73

cardiopulmonary resuscitation (CPR) 107
challenge(s) 1, 8, 9, 13, 15, 24, 25, 28, 45, 46, 47, 48, 49, 50, 51, 52, 53, 54, 94, 95, 96, 97, 100, 101, 102, 104, 109, 114, 116, 117
checklist(s) 107, 108, 120, 121
Cheia 73
coach(es) 3, 8, 15, 37, 55, 58, 59, 61, 64, 68, 70, 73, 81, 82, 83, 96, 107, 119, 120, 122, 123, 124, 125, 126

coach-centred approach 2
coaching context 2, 8, 15, 96
cognitive dimension 55
Cohesion Inventory for Children's
  Sport Team 37
collaboration 42, 43, 49, 73, 76, 82, 84
combat sport(s) 92
combined skill test 107
competence 2, 10, 14, 15, 16, 37, 43,
  44, 63, 107, 115, 116
competition 8, 42, 43, 77, 80, 97, 106,
  122, 125, 126
constraints-led approach 10
constructivism 3
contextualization 2, 3, 7
contextualized sport alphabetization
  model (CSAM) 10
cooperative learning (CL) 113, 117, 119
counter-attack 72
crawl 97, 99, 104
critical thinking 4, 7
croquet 72
culminating event 121, 126
curling 72, 79, 82, 83
curricular adaptations 4, 7, 8
curriculum models 3

darts 72, 73, 75
datchball 73
debate of ideas 9, 12
decision-making 7, 8, 13, 15, 26, 86,
  87, 88, 107, 116
decision making index 88
declarative knowledge 15
decontextualized practice 2, 7, 10, 14
deep (swimming) pool 100, 101, 102, 103
defender(s) 24, 25, 31, 32, 33, 34,
  35, 43
defensive tactical principles 24, 36
developmental games stage model 9,
  12, 59, 60, 61, 62, 63, 65, 70
deweke 73
disabilities 86, 54, 106
Disposition to Cheating in Sports
  Questionnaire 88
dodgeball 73
dorsal flotation 100, 101, 102
drowning 97
Duni 115

emergent models 119
Empowering Sport (ES) 113
empowerment 15, 113
endeavour 118
engagement 1, 112, 115, 118, 119
enjoyment 15, 16, 41, 75, 89, 96, 108,
  114, 115
environmental constraints 10
equipment 10, 11, 13, 27, 43, 60, 75,
  94, 106, 120, 122, 124, 125
equipment manager 77, 122, 124,
  125, 92
exaggeration (of games) 6, 13, 25, 41,
  59, 74, 94
extracurricular context 1, 2, 3, 7, 8, 9,
  62, 73, 96, 97, 113, 119, 120

facilitator 11, 15, 25, 31, 41, 77, 117, 120
fair play 88, 122, 125, 126
Fair Play Scale in Physical Education
  and Sports 88
fakes 74
fear 100
feedback 14, 68, 92, 97, 109, 117,
  122, 124
fidelity protocol(s) 119
filling the bottle 73
first aid 107
fitness 15, 97
floorcurling 82, 83
formal competition 113, 121, 124,
  125, 126
freestyle technique 104
Frisbee 23, 29, 115
futsal 13, 26, 69, 80, 93

game-based approach 4
Game-Centred Approach (GCA) 1, 3,
  4, 5, 6, 10, 11, 12, 13, 14, 15, 29, 35,
  36, 43, 54, 63, 65, 68, 86, 93, 106,
  112, 113, 117, 119, 121
Game-Centred Approach typology
  6, 10
game concept approach 10
game condition 44, 117
game insight approach 10
**Game Performance Assessment
  Instrument (GPAI)** 36, 68, 79, 86,
  87, 88

Analytical index

Game Performance Evaluation Tool (GPET) 36
game performance final index 86, 88, 117
game play 4, 7, 9, 11, 36, 58, 65, 68, 69, 70, 86, 114, 116, 117
game play rubric 69
game practice 7, 10
games concept approach 4, 10
game sense (GS) 3, 8, 45, 55
games taxonomy 6, 7, 9, 72, 73, 92, 93
general checklists 107
global awareness 79, 82, 83, 84
globalization 1
goal 3, 7, 9, 10, 11, 12, 13, 15, 23, 24, 25, 26, 27, 28, 29, 30, 31, 32, 33, 34, 35, 36, 37, 43, 44, 54, 58, 59, 60, 61, 62, 63, 64, 65, 66, 67, 72, 73, 74, 75, 80, 81, 82, 83, 84, 94, 95, 98, 100, 102, 104, 114, 117, 118, 124
goalkeeper 24, 26, 27, 28, 31, 32, 33, 34, 35
golf 72, 74
GROW strategy 12

handball 6, 27, 80, 84, 116
health-based physical education 119
hockey 24
holistic personal development 10, 54
hybridization(s) 112, 113, 114, 119, 120, 121, 122
hydrodynamics 106

implementation 1, 2, 4, 65, 66, 103, 112, 113, 116, 119, 120, 121, 126
implication of the game index 86, 88
inclusion 3, 7, 73
indirect competition 96
individual games/sports 6, 92, 93, 94, 95, 96, 97, 106, 107
individual games assessment 106
individual games with cooperation 93
individual games without cooperation 92
individual playing 23, 59
information and communication technology (ICT) 1
inquiry-based strategy 4, 5, 7, 8, 11, 12, 79, 81

instructional models 3
instructor 2, 9, 10, 11, 12, 13, 14, 25, 26, 27, 30, 36, 42, 43, 44, 58, 59, 60, 62, 63, 66, 70, 73, 74, 75, 76, 77, 78, 79, 80, 84, 86, 88, 92, 96, 97, 100, 102, 103, 104, 106, 107, 109, 114
intellectual disability 86
International Swimming Federation (FINA) 100, 102, 104
interviews 107
invasion/territory games 6, 14, 15, 23, 25, 26, 27, 28, 35, 36, 37, 94, 114, 115
invasion games assessment 36
invasion games competence model (IGCM) 10, 116, 121
Ironman triathlon 92

javelin 92, 94, 95
journaling 107

knowledge 2, 4, 6, 8, 14, 30, 36, 66, 89, 107, 112, 117, 119, 120, 122, 126

lacrosse 27
learners 8, 11, 13, 14, 23, 25, 28, 29, 30, 37, 40, 41, 42, 43, 44, 54, 55, 59, 60, 61, 62, 63, 74, 75, 76, 77, 86, 89, 92, 93, 94, 95, 96, 97, 100, 101, 102, 103, 104, 106, 107, 109, 112, 114, 118, 120, 121, 122, 123, 126
learners' perceptions 15, 36, 37, 113, 115
learning outcomes 8, 14, 25, 26, 74, 94, 112, 120
life-saving skills 97
literacy 2, 7, 14, 15, 16, 41, 78

maintain ball possession 24
matangululu 73
mediation 117, 122
Model Athletic Assessment Tool (MAAT) 106
models-based practice (MsBP) 112
modified games 4, 5, 6, 8, 9, 10, 13, 16, 25, 26, 27, 30, 35, 36, 37, 41, 42, 58, 59, 60, 62, 64, 65, 66, 74, 75, 77, 78, 79, 80, 81, 82, 83, 85, 93, 94, 114, 121

Analytical index   133

motivation 2, 3, 10, 12, 15, 16, 72, 103, 115
motor patterns 10, 13, 14, 15, 36, 54, 92, 106
moving target games 73, 74, 79, 84, 88

net/wall games 6, 40, 41, 42, 43, 44, 54, 55, 94, 114
net/wall games assessment 54
non-lineal pedagogy 10
novice 62, 63, 106
number of players 6, 10, 13, 26, 41, 42, 59, 60, 74, 75, 94

offensive tactical principles 24
off-the-ball players 23, 24, 26, 28, 30, 32, 36, 37, 68
on-the-ball players 23, 24, 28, 30, 31, 68
opponent(s) 37, 40, 41, 43, 44, 45, 50, 53, 54, 59, 74, 83
opposed target games 72, 73, 79, 82
opposition 73, 76, 82, 83, 84
organization 77, 116, 118
orientation 73, 76, 80, 82
outcomes 8, 14, 25, 26, 29, 74, 94, 106, 112, 119, 120
outdoor individual sports 92, 93

Paralympic sports 79, 83
pedagogical models 3, 55, 112, 113, 114, 117, 119, 120
pedagogical principles 11
perceived competence 16, 37, 115
Perceived Game-Specific Competence Scale 37
performance 7, 8, 14, 15, 26, 27, 36, 38, 55, 56, 62, 68, 69, 77, 78, 79, 86, 88, 92, 93, 95, 97, 106, 107, 108, 116, 117, 119, 121, 126
period of adaptation 102
petanque 72, 79, 83, 84
physical activity guideline 1
physical disability 86
physical education 1, 3, 8, 14, 15, 37, 62, 73, 88, 112, 113, 116, 119
physical literacy 2, 14, 15, 16, 36, 41
pitcher 61, 62, 63, 64, 65, 66, 67
player(s) 2, 3, 4, 5, 6, 8, 9, 10, 11, 12, 13, 15, 16, 23, 24, 25, 26, 27, 28, 29, 30, 31, 32, 35, 36, 37, 40, 41, 42, 43, 44, 45, 46, 47, 48, 49, 50, 51, 52, 53, 54, 55, 58, 59, 60, 63, 65, 68, 72, 73, 74, 75, 80, 82, 83, 84, 85, 87, 92, 94, 104, 116, 117, 120, 122, 123, 124, 125, 126
player-coach 122, 123, 124, 126
playing area 10, 13, 26, 27, 31, 32, 33, 34, 35, 40, 41, 42, 43, 45, 46, 47, 48, 49, 50, 51, 52, 53, 54, 59, 60, 75, 80, 83, 94, 106
play practice (PP) 8, 92, 96, 97, 98, 102, 103, 106
position 23, 24, 28, 29, 32, 40, 41, 45, 47, 48, 49, 53, 55, 59, 61, 63, 65, 67, 69, 73, 74, 75, 80, 81, 82, 83, 84, 86, 87, 93, 95, 97, 98, 100, 101, 102, 103, 108
possession 23, 24, 26, 27, 29, 30, 31, 36, 40
power 65, 73, 74, 76, 80, 83, 86, 87
practitioner 116
pre-season 115, 123, 124
principles 6, 9, 11, 15, 36, 40, 41, 58, 60, 63, 66, 72, 73, 74, 76, 79, 82, 84, 92, 95, 96, 106, 116
projectile 23, 24, 29, 72, 73, 74, 75, 76, 77, 86
projectile placement 73
protection 73, 76, 82, 84
psychological factors 12, 97

questioning strategies 4, 5, 7, 8, 11, 12, 16, 27, 28, 43, 60, 62, 75, 78, 95, 115, 122
question intonation 12

race 93, 94, 95, 100, 103, 104
racket 40, 45, 46, 47, 48, 50, 52, 53
representation (of games) 6, 13, 25, 41, 58, 74, 94
researcher(s) 112, 113, 119
resource(s) 89
responsibility 3, 11, 12, 55, 113, 114, 117, 118, 123, 124, 126
rubric(s) 68, 69, 70
rubric for assessing badminton 54
rules 6, 10, 11, 13, 15, 24, 25, 26, 41, 42, 44, 59, 62, 66, 72, 74, 75, 79, 94, 96

scenarios 55, 107, 108
school 1, 7, 62, 66, 73, 114, 116
score 6, 13, 23, 24, 27, 28, 29, 30, 31, 32, 34, 35, 40, 43, 44, 45, 48, 49, 50, 51, 52, 53, 54, 55, 58, 59, 60, 61, 63, 64, 65, 67, 68, 72, 74, 75, 80, 81, 83, 84, 86, 94, 95, 96, 115, 126
score and/or goal 27, 43, 60, 75, 95
season 8, 116, 117, 121, 122, 123
self-assessment 14
self-confidence 12, 37
self-determination index 3
self-esteem 37
shallow pool 100, 101, 102
shootball 79, 84, 85, 87
shuttle 45, 46, 47, 48, 49, 50, 51, 52, 53, 54
skill development 9, 14, 15, 54, 106, 113
skill execution index 88
skill(s) level 70, 80, 118, 119, 122
skill testing 14, 107
small-sided and conditioned game(s) (SSCG(s)) 6, 9, 11, 13, 35, 42, 64, 77, 112, 123
soccer 6, 8, 24, 26, 29, 30, 36, 37, 92, 116
social dimension 37, 55, 70, 88, 107
social interaction 11, 15
softball 58, 59, 61, 62, 63, 64, 65, 66, 69
sport education (SE) 55, 96, 112, 113, 114, 115, 116, 117, 119
Sport Education Tactical Model (SETM) 115, 116, 121
Sport for Peace curriculum 112
sport literacy 7, 78
sport pedagogy 1, 92
step-game-approach (SGA) 112, 117, 121
striking/fielding games 6, 58, 59, 60, 61, 62, 63, 68, 73, 94, 114
striking/fielding games assessment 68
stroke 94, 95, 97, 98, 99, 104
structural elements 10, 114, 115
student-centred approaches 3, 4, 11, 114, 115, 117, 118, 119
student-coach(es) 116, 117
students 11, 12, 15, 44, 55, 60, 62, 63, 65, 68, 103, 112, 113, 114, 115, 116, 117, 118, 119, 120

summative assessment 14, 86, 106
supportive climate 86
swimming 97, 98, 99, 100, 101, 102, 103, 104, 106, 107, 108, 109
swimming style(s) 97, 98, 99, 104
syllabus 63, 73

tactical and technical dimension 68, 86
tactical awareness 7, 8, 15, 28, 44, 60, 75, 77, 78, 79, 80, 81, 83, 95, 124
tactical complexity 6, 7, 9, 13, 26, 29, 30, 42, 62, 76
tactical-decision learning model (T-DLM) 9
tactical games approach (TGA) 7, 8, 23, 29, 30, 37, 114, 115, 116, 118, 120, 121, 123, 124, 125, 126
tactical knowledge 36, 66, 107, 122
tactical problem 4, 7, 8, 13, 25, 29, 30, 41, 42, 44, 45, 62, 65, 66, 70, 76, 77, 78, 114, 123, 124, 125
tactical-technical element(s) 1, 5, 6, 9, 58, 59, 61, 62, 65, 68, 72, 76, 78, 79, 81, 82, 84, 88, 92
tactical-technical level 29, 30, 55, 61, 62, 68, 69, 70, 72, 76, 80, 118, 119, 120, 122
tactical understanding 116
tactics and strategies 11, 13, 15, 23, 26, 62, 77, 79, 95, 96, 114, 115, 116, 123
target 6, 7, 23, 29, 30, 31, 32, 69, 72, 73, 74, 75, 76, 77, 79, 80, 82, 83, 86, 85, 86, 87, 88
target games 6, 72, 73, 74, 75, 76, 77, 78, 79, 80, 84, 86, 88, 94
target games assessment 86
target players 29, 30, 31, 32, 73
task constraints 10
tchoukball 26
teach backs 107
teacher(s) 7, 58, 59, 64, 68, 70, 73, 96, 107, 113, 114, 115, 116, 117, 118, 119
Teaching Games for Understanding (TGfU) 3, 4, 6, 7, 8, 9, 72, 77, 78, 79, 113, 114, 115, 116, 121
teaching personal and social responsibility (TPSR) 119
teammate(s) 3, 23, 24, 28, 29, 33, 37, 47, 61, 66, 68, 73, 74, 79, 85, 93, 94, 95, 102, 106, 117, 125

Team Sport Assessment Procedure
 (TSAP) 36
teamwork 3, 16, 23
technical awareness 30, 79, 81, 82
technical development 2, 15, 97
technical gestures 78, 79, 82
technical skills 2, 8, 36, 40, 62, 66, 72,
 76, 77, 79, 81, 84, 85, 92, 96, 97,
 107, 122, 124, 125
tennis 40, 42, 93, 118, 120
theoretical test 107
throw/hit selection 73, 76
traditional approaches 2, 3, 4, 6, 7, 14,
 95, 112, 115, 121
trajectory 73, 76
transference 1, 6, 15

Analytical index 135

ultimate 27, 29, 115
unopposed target games 72, 73, 77, 79,
 80, 84

ventral flotation 100, 102, 103
volleyball 115, 40, 41, 42, 45, 54,
 115, 117

water competence 107
well-being 37, 97
wheelchair 36, 63, 68, 79
World Health Organization (WHO) 1
wrestling sports 93

young learners 11, 25, 28, 76, 86, 94,
 96, 126

Practical sessions index

hybridization practical application with tactical games approach and sport education 120

individual games practical application with play practice 96

invasion games practical application with tactical games approach 29

net/wall games practical application with game sense 45

striking/fielding games practical application with developmental game stage model 61

target games practical application with teaching games for understanding 77

For Product Safety Concerns and Information please contact our EU
representative GPSR@taylorandfrancis.com
Taylor & Francis Verlag GmbH, Kaufingerstraße 24, 80331 München, Germany

www.ingramcontent.com/pod-product-compliance
Lightning Source LLC
Chambersburg PA
CBHW051102230426
43667CB00013B/2411